FAVORITE
COOKIES

Photographs **Annabelle Breakey**

weldon**owen**

Gingerbread People
(page 85)

contents

COOKIE BASICS

What could be better than the aroma of freshly baked cookies coming from the oven? Perhaps only the first sublime bite of a warm chocolate chip cookie with its melted chocolate bits—a moment of pure delight. Cookies evoke so many wonderful emotions; they fill your kitchen with the aromas of childhood and the memories of holiday time. Nothing is more satisfying than dipping a hand into the cookie jar to instantly indulge your sweet tooth.

The recipes in this book begin with our favorite selection of classic and versatile drop cookies, perfect for any day of the year. Serving these fresh from the oven, like Salted-Caramel Chocolate Chip Cookies (page 38), will elicit instant smiles. Next come recipes for indulgent bars and tender, buttery sandwich cookies that are all wonderful alternatives to serving cupcakes at parties. Try your hand at Homemade Oreos (page 43) for kids (or kids at heart). And finally, 17 festive holiday cookies bring to life dreams of peppermint, gingerbread, rugelach, and a winter wonderland of flavors.

The secret to successful cookie baking starts with the dough, so in the next few pages we cover everything from equipment essentials to rolling, cutting, and shaping dough. Cookie decorating is easily doable with a few basic tools and our handy how-tos. Many of these recipes are simple enough to make that you can enlist little hands to help. And don't miss our tips for proper storing and beautiful gift giving.

We celebrate the cookie and all of its different textures—crispy, chewy, or downright gooey—and encourage you to experiment with your favorite flavors and ideas for mix-ins. You'll find exciting flavor variations throughout, from Matcha Shortbread Cookies (page 75) to Honey & Rose Water Mexican Wedding Cookies (page 94). Perhaps you'll find a new favorite or develop a new holiday tradition. Get creative with whatever shapes, colors, and designs you like. Just don't forget a big glass of cold milk.

spritz cookies

chuck's madeleines

lemon & black
pepper sugar cookies

chocolate
pretzel–peanut butter
sandwich cookies

peanut butter cookies

peppermint candy
cookies

classic alfajores

seven–layer bars

butterscotch, coconut &
macadamia nut cookies

snickerdoodles

blackberry-pecan
Thumbprints

lemon bars

linzer cookies

perfect chocolate chip cookies

mexican
wedding cookies

chocolate crinkle cookies

chocolate florentines

homemade oreos

COOKIE BASICS

There are several types of cookies—dropped, rolled and cut, pressed, and sandwich—and we love them all. While many do not require any special tools, some might need a specific pan or piece of equipment.

Tool Kit

In addition to the standard suite of baking tools (mixing bowls, measuring cups, and baking sheets), it's good to have a few other items on hand before you get started.

An electric stand mixer is handy for mixing dough, and wire cooling racks are essential for allowing air circulation so that cookies cool quickly and evenly.

Use parchment paper or silicone baking mats to line baking sheets to prevent dough from sticking. And, of course, a rolling pin and a selection of cookie cutters are a must for making Christmas cookies!

For decorating, be sure to have an offset spatula (also called a palette knife) on hand, as well as a piping bag and an array of tips (see page 14 for detailed decorating instructions). Gather several small bowls (dishwasher-safe materials make cleanup a breeze) for mixing icing. Small paintbrushes to spread icing, paint designs, and brush on luster dust are also useful.

You'll need a cookie press for our Spritz Cookies (page 90) and a special madeleine pan for Chuck Williams' own recipe for madeleines (page 70).

Ingredients

Most cookie recipes use the same stockpile of ingredients: butter, flour, sugar, eggs, and vanilla or other flavorings. Using the highest quality of each yields the best results. Start out with all your ingredients at room temperature, unless the recipe instructs otherwise. The temperature of the butter is important: if the butter is too cold, it will not fluff up or cream properly, and if it is too warm or nearly melted, it will be too thin to fluff up at all.

Measuring

Professional bakers use a kitchen scale to measure dry ingredients, but most home cooks use cups and spoons. Whichever method you use, be sure to measure precisely and use the same method for the entire recipe.

Serving

From a cookie jar brimming with chocolate chip cookies to a vintage tray stacked with brownies, presentation ideas are endless. Keep in mind that some recipes have specific serving instructions; for example, madeleines are best served warm from the oven, dusted with confectioners' sugar.

COOKIE CARE 101

Cookie dough and finished cookies are delicate. It is important to handle cookies with care at every stage of the process—from prepping, rolling, and cutting to cooling, decorating, and storing.

Shaping & Freezing

Making great cookies starts with the dough. Temperature is key! For best results, follow the instructions in each recipe regarding chilling and wrapping cookie dough; many require refrigerating the dough for at least 1 hour or up to overnight. Rolled cookie dough should never get too warm or it will spread while baking. When making Spritz Cookies (page 90), be sure that the dough is at room temperature as it needs to be soft enough to extrude easily from the cookie press. To save time, the dough for some recipes can be prepared ahead and then frozen, as with the Checkerboard Cookies (page 81). If working with frozen dough, let it stand at room temperature for a few minutes before shaping or slicing.

Baking & Cooling

Oven temperatures vary, and since cookies have short baking times, it is important to watch them closely so they don't burn. Check for doneness a couple of minutes before the recipe indicates. To ensure even cooking, rotate the baking sheets halfway through the baking time. Use wire racks for cooling; they allow air to circulate beneath the cookies, which helps them cool quickly and evenly. When making bar cookies, use the size of dish called for in the recipe—using a different size will change the baking time and may affect the texture.

Storing & Packaging

Most cookies will keep well in an airtight container, layered between sheets of parchment paper, at room temperature for a few days. To pack bar treats for picnics and parties, wrap them individually in aluminum foil or waxed paper. A dozen beautifully baked cookies can easily become the perfect hostess or holiday gift. Wrap cookies in waxed paper and place on colorful tissue paper in a sturdy decorative box or metal tin, then tie with festive ribbon.

Troubleshooting

- **The cookies spread too much during baking.** The butter was too soft when added, or the dough was placed on a hot baking sheet.

- **The cookies are burned on the bottom.** The cookies were too thin, the oven was too hot, the baking sheet was too thin or placed too low in the oven, or the baking sheets were not rotated during baking.

- **The cookies did not bake evenly.** The baking sheets were not rotated during baking.

- **The cookies fell apart when removed from the baking sheet.** The cookies were removed from the baking sheet too soon.

- **The cookies stuck to the baking sheet.** The cookies were not baked long enough or were left too long on the baking sheet.

DECORATING PRIMER

While making cookie dough is a science, decorating cookies is definitely an art! So let your creative side shine through (perhaps with a little luster dust), and use our guide to help inspire your masterful creations.

Royal Icing

It all begins with royal icing. This stiff white icing, made from confectioners' sugar and egg whites or meringue powder, got its name after it was used to ice Queen Victoria's white wedding cake celebrating her marriage to Prince Albert in 1840. (See recipe, facing page.)

Equipment

A pastry bag (made from cloth or sturdy plastic) with an assortment of removable tips ranging in sizes, a silicone spatula, and a small offset spatula will make easy work of decorating.

Food Coloring

Liquids, powders, and gels are all used to tint icings and frostings. Gel food coloring is the most concentrated and therefore creates colors that are more vibrant. Also, it won't thin the icing as much as liquid food coloring, which yields colors that are more pastel-toned. You can use a toothpick to add gel food coloring into the icing bit by bit until you are happy with the color. Start light—a little gel goes a long way, and it is easier to add more coloring than it is to lighten up a dark icing.

 TIP *Always have extra icing on hand to lighten up a color that became too dark or to remake a color that isn't right.*

Filling a Pastry Bag

Piping tips for pastry bags are available in a variety of sizes and shapes (most common are plain and fluted). The smaller the number, the smaller the hole, but numbering systems vary slightly by brand.

To fill the pastry bag, firmly push the desired decorating tip down into the small hole in the pastry bag. If you're using a device called a coupler to hold the tip in place, screw it on tightly. Next, form a cuff by folding down the top one-third of the bag. Place one hand under the cuff. Using a silicone spatula, scoop icing into the bag with the other hand to no more than half full. Then unfold the cuff and push the icing down toward the tip, forcing out any air bubbles, and twist the bag closed where the icing ends. With your dominant hand, hold the bag where you just made the twist. With your nondominant hand, hold the bag near the tip, to help stabilize it, and proceed to pipe.

Piping & Flooding

Bakers use terms like "piping" and "flooding" when giving instructions for decorating cookies. Piping creates an outline at the edge of the cookie and flooding fills in the outline with icing. You can use the same bowl of white or colored royal icing for both. Scoop out about one-third of the icing into a piping bag for piping, and thin the remaining icing slightly for flooding.

Piping, flooding, and decorating are easy ways to add an elegant finishing touch to your cookies.

- **To pipe:** Fit your desired tip into a pastry bag and then fill it with royal icing. Pipe a line of icing as close to the edge of the cookie as possible. Let the outline dry for a few minutes before you begin flooding. Or, skip the flooding and just use the piping bag and some decorations to create your finished design.

- **To flood:** Thin the royal icing slightly by adding warm water 1 teaspoon at a time until it is just spreadable but not runny. Then use an offset spatula, a small paintbrush, or the back of a spoon to spread enough icing over the cookie to cover it generously. Check the icing for air bubbles and pop any with a toothpick. Let the cookies dry completely before storing or packaging.

TIP *To keep the icing from drying out while you're decorating the cookies, cover the bowls of colored icing with plastic wrap when you're not using them, or place a damp towel over the electric-mixer bowl that contains the uncolored royal icing.*

Decorations

There are endless choices for decorations, enough to make every cookie unique. A sprinkling of sanding sugar (also called colored sugar crystals) is a simple way to make cookies sparkle, and rainbow nonpareils lend playfulness to any design. Dragées—tiny beads commonly available in silver, gold, and other metallic hues—add instant glamour to any cookie. Luster dust gives a metallic sheen to your icing; mix the powder with a flavoring extract and apply it with a small, clean paintbrush.

ROYAL ICING

4 cups (1 lb/500 g) confectioners' sugar

3 tablespoons meringue powder

½ teaspoon extract, such as vanilla or almond (optional)

Makes about 3 cups (24 fl oz/750 ml)

In a large bowl, combine the confectioners' sugar, meringue powder, ½ cup (125 ml) warm water, and extract (if using). Using an electric mixer on medium speed, beat until the mixture is fluffy yet dense, 7–8 minutes. To thin the icing, use a silicone spatula to stir in more warm water, 1 teaspoon at a time. To test the consistency, drizzle a spoonful of icing into the bowl; a ribbon should remain on the surface for about 5 seconds. Cover and refrigerate airtight for up to 1 week. Stir vigorously just before using.

TIPS FOR ROLLING & CUTTING DOUGH

The first few times you work with cookie dough can be tricky. But like other rewarding baking adventures, practice makes perfect—especially if you follow these handy tips.

- When rolling out dough, work quickly so that it doesn't become too warm. This will help ensure that the cutout shapes don't spread when they bake. If your kitchen is warm, refrigerate the cutout cookies on a baking sheet for 15 to 20 minutes before putting them in the oven.

- Flour your work surface and rolling pin before getting started. Or, if the dough becomes too sticky and tricky, roll it between sheets of waxed or parchment paper.

- Dip cookie cutters in flour before pressing them into the dough, and place cookie cutters as close to the edge of the rolled-out dough so you can cut out as many cookies as possible and minimize scraps.

- If dough scraps become sticky, refrigerate them for 10 minutes before rerolling. (And resist the temptation to roll the same piece of dough more than twice.)

- If you can't find the right cookie cutter, trace or print your favorite design on card stock and cut it out with scissors. Then place this template directly on the rolled-out dough and cut out shapes with the tip of a paring knife.

- For special occasions, make a big impact by using cookie cutters in the same shape but in an assortment of sizes. Try this with Gingerbread People (page 85) during the holidays. Be sure to group similar sizes together on separate sheets so they bake evenly.

DROP COOKIES

Peanut Butter Cookies

Don't worry if all you have on hand is chunky peanut butter. This easy recipe will still work fine. To give these old-fashioned cookies a decorative finish, bake and cool them as directed, then use a spoonful of melted chocolate of your choice to fill in the grooves created by the fork tines.

1⅓ cups (7 oz/220 g)
all-purpose flour

½ teaspoon baking powder

½ teaspoon baking soda

½ teaspoon kosher salt

½ cup (4 oz/125 g) unsalted butter, melted and cooled

½ cup (4 oz/125 g) granulated sugar

½ cup (3½ oz/105 g) firmly packed light brown sugar

1 cup (10 oz/315 g) creamy peanut butter

1 large egg

1 teaspoon pure vanilla extract

Makes about 20 cookies

1 In a bowl, sift together the flour, baking powder, baking soda, and salt. Set aside.

2 In the bowl of a stand mixer fitted with the paddle attachment, beat together the butter, granulated sugar, brown sugar, peanut butter, egg, and vanilla on low speed until well combined, about 3 minutes. Stop the mixer and scrape down the sides of the bowl. Add the flour mixture and beat on low speed until combined, about 1 minute. Cover the bowl and refrigerate until the dough is firm, about 2 hours.

3 Preheat the oven to 350°F (180°C). Line a baking sheet with parchment paper.

4 Shape the dough into 1-inch (2.5-cm) balls and place on the prepared baking sheet, spacing the cookies about 2 inches (5 cm) apart. Using the tines of a fork dipped in flour, flatten each ball slightly and make a pattern of parallel indentations.

5 Bake until the cookies are golden brown, 10–12 minutes. Transfer the baking sheet to a wire rack and let the cookies cool on the sheet for 3 minutes, then transfer the cookies to the rack and let cool slightly before serving.

 To measure the peanut butter, spray a measuring cup with nonstick cooking spray, then spoon the peanut butter into it. The peanut butter will slip out of the measuring cup easily, and the measuring cup will clean up effortlessly.

Butterscotch, Coconut & Macadamia Nut Cookies

Rich, sweet butterscotch chips partner perfectly with the buttery, creamy flavor and crisp crunch of macadamia nuts. But another flavor of chips—semisweet, milk, or white chocolate or even peanut butter—can stand in for the butterscotch. For a delicious variation, trade out the macadamia nuts for walnuts or pecans.

1⅓ cups (7 oz/220 g) all-purpose flour

½ teaspoon baking powder

½ teaspoon baking soda

½ teaspoon kosher salt

½ cup (4 oz/125 g) unsalted butter, at room temperature

½ cup (4 oz/125 g) granulated sugar

½ cup (3½ oz/105 g) firmly packed light brown sugar

1 large egg

½ teaspoon pure vanilla extract

1¼ cups (5 oz/155 g) shredded dried sweetened coconut

½ cup (3 oz/90 g) butterscotch chips

¾ cup (3¾ oz/115 g) macadamia nuts, roughly chopped

Makes about 20 cookies

1 Preheat the oven to 325°F (165°C). Line a baking sheet with parchment paper.

2 In a bowl, sift together the flour, baking powder, baking soda, and salt. Set aside.

3 In the bowl of a stand mixer fitted with the paddle attachment, beat together the butter, granulated sugar, and brown sugar on medium speed until light and fluffy, about 3 minutes. Reduce the speed to low, add the egg and vanilla, and beat until combined, about 1 minute. Stop the mixer and scrape down the sides of the bowl. Add the flour mixture and beat on low speed until combined, about 1 minute. Stop the mixer and fold in the coconut, butterscotch chips, and macadamia nuts.

4 Drop the dough by rounded tablespoons onto the prepared baking sheet, spacing the cookies about 2 inches (5 cm) apart.

5 Bake until the cookies are golden brown, 16–18 minutes. Transfer the cookies to a wire rack and let cool completely.

 TIP *These cookies will satisfy any sweet tooth. If you want to tone down the sugar, use unsweetened coconut.*

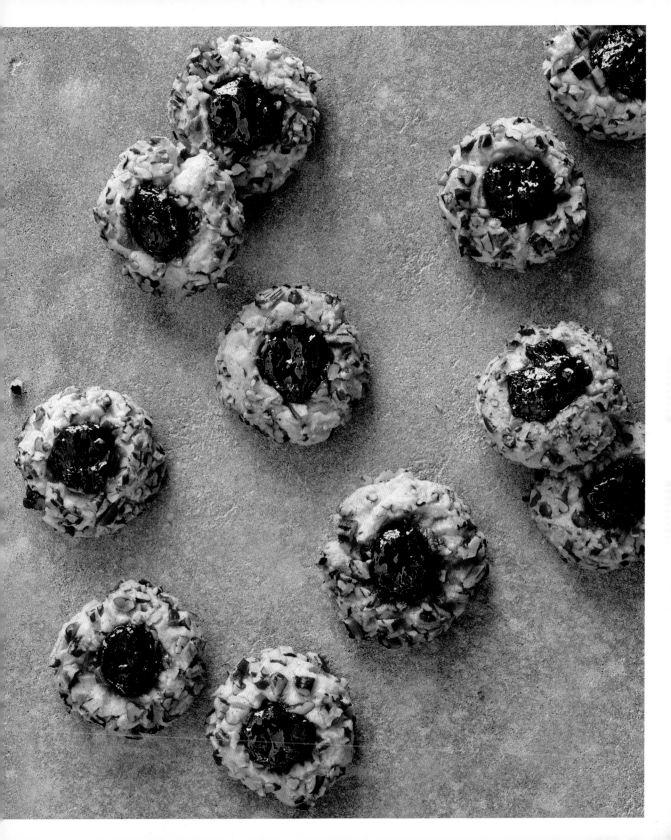

Blackberry-Pecan Thumbprints

Buttery, tender, and a bit crumbly, thumbprint cookies are a colorful addition to any cookie plate. For variety, fill half of the cookies with raspberry jam. And if you like, use blanched almonds instead of pecans and add ½ teaspoon almond extract with the vanilla extract. If the dough is too soft to shape easily, refrigerate it for 30 minutes to 1 hour and try again.

2 cups (10 oz/315 g)
all-purpose flour

¼ teaspoon kosher salt

1 cup (8 oz/250 g) unsalted butter,
at room temperature

½ cup (4 oz/125 g) sugar

1 large egg yolk

1 teaspoon pure vanilla extract

1 cup (4 oz/125 g) finely chopped
pecans

¼ cup (2½ oz/75 g) blackberry jam

1 cup (4 oz/125 g) fresh blackberries
(optional)

Makes about 2 dozen cookies

1 Preheat the oven to 325°F (165°C). Line a baking sheet with parchment paper.

2 In a bowl, sift together the flour and salt. Set aside.

3 In the bowl of a stand mixer fitted with the paddle attachment, beat together the butter and sugar on medium speed until light and fluffy, about 3 minutes. Reduce the speed to low, add the egg yolk and vanilla, and beat until combined, about 1 minute. Stop the mixer and scrape down the sides of the bowl. Add the flour mixture and beat on low speed until combined, about 1 minute.

4 Place the pecans in a small bowl. Scoop up a rounded tablespoon of the dough and roll between your palms into a ball. Lightly roll the ball in the pecans to coat completely and place on the prepared baking sheet. Repeat with the remaining dough, spacing the cookies about 2 inches (5 cm) apart. Using a thumb, press an indentation about ¼ inch (6 mm) deep in the center of each cookie. Spoon about ½ teaspoon of the jam into each indentation and top with a blackberry, if using.

5 Bake until the cookies are lightly browned on the bottoms and edges, 20–25 minutes. Transfer the baking sheet to a wire rack and let the cookies cool on the sheet for 5 minutes, then transfer the cookies to the rack and let cool completely.

 Add a twist to these cookies in the summer by mixing and matching your favorite jams and fresh berries.

Oatmeal-Raisin Cookies

Old-fashioned rolled oats yield the chewy texture and rustic look that many bakers—and eaters—associate with the best oatmeal cookies. If you prefer a more delicate cookie with a finer texture, substitute quick-cooking oats. Don't use instant oats, as they are typically too powdery to provide the dough with the necessary structure.

2 cups (10 oz/315 g)
all-purpose flour

1 teaspoon baking powder

½ teaspoon baking soda

½ teaspoon kosher salt

3 teaspoons ground cinnamon

½ teaspoon ground nutmeg

1 cup (8 oz/250 g) unsalted butter,
at room temperature

¾ cup (6 oz/185 g) granulated
sugar

¾ cup (6 oz/185 g) firmly packed
light brown sugar

2 large eggs

1½ teaspoons pure vanilla extract

2½ cups (7½ oz/235 g) rolled oats

2½ cups (15 oz/470 g) raisins

Makes about 3 dozen cookies

1 Preheat the oven to 375°F (190°C). Line a baking sheet with parchment paper.

2 In a bowl, sift together the flour, baking powder, baking soda, salt, cinnamon, and nutmeg. Set aside.

3 In the bowl of a stand mixer fitted with the paddle attachment, beat together the butter, granulated sugar, and brown sugar on medium speed until light and fluffy, about 3 minutes. Reduce the speed to low and add the eggs one a time, beating well after each addition. Add the vanilla and beat until combined, about 1 minute. Stop the mixer and scrape down the sides of the bowl. Add the flour mixture and beat on low speed until combined, about 1 minute. Stop the mixer and stir in the oats and raisins, distributing them evenly throughout the dough.

4 Drop the dough by rounded tablespoons onto the prepared baking sheet, spacing the cookies about 2 inches (5 cm) apart. Flatten each ball gently with the palm of your hand.

5 Bake until the cookies are golden brown, 9–11 minutes. Transfer the baking sheet to a wire rack and let the cookies cool on the sheet for 3 minutes, then transfer the cookies to the rack and let cool slightly before serving.

TIP *For a more sophisticated take on the classic cookie, swap the raisins for roughly chopped dates. Or, for the ultimate crowd-pleaser, omit the dried fruit and stir in chocolate chips and walnuts instead.*

Cowboy Cookies

Despite their name, these ingredient-packed cookies, which boast the texture and flavor of old-fashioned oatmeal cookies, appeal to more than denizens of the Wild West. If you have time, refrigerate the dough for 30 minutes to 1 hour before or after shaping to prevent the cookies from spreading too much in the hot oven.

1½ cups (7 ½ oz/235 g) all-purpose flour

2 teaspoons baking powder

1 teaspoon baking soda

1 teaspoon ground cinnamon

½ teaspoon kosher salt

¾ cup (6 oz/185 g) unsalted butter, at room temperature

¾ cup (6 oz/185 g) granulated sugar

¾ cup (6 oz/185 g) firmly packed dark brown sugar

2 large eggs

2 teaspoons pure vanilla extract

1 cup (6 oz/185 g) semisweet chocolate chips

2 cups (6 oz/185 g) rolled oats

¾ cup (3 oz/90 g) shredded dried unsweetened coconut

½ cup (2 oz/60 g) chopped walnuts

Makes about 2 dozen cookies

1 Preheat the oven to 350°F (180°C). Line a baking sheet with parchment paper.

2 In a bowl, sift together the flour, baking powder, baking soda, cinnamon, and salt. Set aside.

3 In the bowl of a stand mixer fitted with the paddle attachment, beat together the butter, granulated sugar, and brown sugar on medium speed until light and fluffy, about 3 minutes. Reduce the speed to low, add the eggs one at a time, beating well after each addition. Add the vanilla and beat until combined, about 1 minute. Stop the mixer and scrape down the sides of the bowl. Add the flour mixture and beat on low speed until combined, about 1 minute. Stop the mixer and stir in the chocolate chips, oats, coconut, and walnuts.

4 Drop the dough by rounded tablespoons onto the prepared baking sheet, spacing the cookies about 3 inches (7.5 cm) apart.

5 Bake until the cookies are golden brown, 15–17 minutes. Transfer the cookies to a wire rack and let cool completely.

Chocolate Florentines

A successful almond Florentine—lacy, thin, crisp—depends on achieving the perfect balance between the batter and the almonds. The batter should bind the nuts without burying them. Work quickly after removing the batter from the heat because it will stiffen as it cools. Although the chocolate glaze is classic, the cookies are delicious without it.

FOR THE COOKIES

1 teaspoon grated orange zest

¼ cup (1½ oz/45 g)
all-purpose flour

5 tablespoons (2½ oz/75 g)
unsalted butter, cut into pieces

¼ cup (60 ml) heavy cream

½ cup (4 oz/125 g) sugar

2 tablespoons honey

¾ cup (3 oz/90 g) sliced blanched
almonds

FOR THE CHOCOLATE GLAZE

6 oz (185 g) semisweet chocolate,
finely chopped

½ cup (4 oz/125 g) unsalted butter

1 tablespoon light corn syrup

Makes about 2 dozen cookies

1 To make the cookies, preheat the oven to 325°F (165°C). Line 2 baking sheets with parchment paper.

2 In a small bowl, stir together the orange zest and flour until the zest is coated. Set aside.

3 In a saucepan over low heat, combine the butter, cream, sugar, and honey. Cook, stirring, until the butter melts and the sugar dissolves. Raise the heat to medium-high and bring to a boil, stirring constantly, then boil for 2 minutes. Remove from the heat and stir in the almonds, followed by the flour mixture. The batter will be thick. Drop the batter by 2-teaspoon scoops onto the prepared baking sheets, spacing the cookies about 3 inches (7.5 cm) apart. Flatten each cookie with the back of the spoon.

4 Bake the cookies, 1 sheet at a time, until they spread to about 3 inches (7.5 cm), are bubbling vigorously, and have light brown edges, 8–10 minutes. Transfer the baking sheets to wire racks and let the cookies cool on the sheets for 10 minutes. Using a wide spatula, transfer them to the racks and let cool completely.

5 To make the chocolate glaze, place the chocolate, butter, and corn syrup in a large heatproof bowl set over (but not touching) barely simmering water in a saucepan and heat, stirring often, until the chocolate and butter are melted, about 4 minutes. Remove from the heat and pour the glaze through a fine-mesh sieve into a bowl. Let cool to 92°F (33°C) before using.

6 Using a spoon, drizzle the chocolate glaze over the top of each cookie. Let stand until the glaze sets, about 30 minutes.

Snickerdoodles

When you bake these cookies, your kitchen will fill with the heady aroma of cinnamon. The best versions of this sugar-cookie relative emerge pillowy at the center and golden and slightly crisp at the edges. Once cooled, they are deliciously chewy and perfect for dipping into a glass of milk.

2 ½ cups (12 ½ oz/390 g) all-purpose flour

2 teaspoons cream of tartar

1 teaspoon baking soda

¼ teaspoon kosher salt

½ cup (4 oz/125 g) unsalted butter, at room temperature

¼ lb (125 g) vegetable shortening, at room temperature

2 cups (1 lb/500 g) sugar

2 large eggs

¼ cup (1 oz/30 g) ground cinnamon

Makes about 2 dozen cookies

1 Preheat the oven to 350°F (180°C). Line a baking sheet with parchment paper.

2 In a bowl, sift together the flour, cream of tartar, baking soda, and salt. Set aside.

3 In the bowl of a stand mixer fitted with the paddle attachment, beat together the butter, shortening, and 1½ cups (12 oz/375 g) of the sugar on medium speed until light and fluffy, about 3 minutes. Reduce the speed to low, add the eggs, and beat until combined, about 1 minute. Stop the mixer and scrape down the sides of the bowl. Add the flour mixture and beat on low speed until combined, about 1 minute.

4 In a small bowl, stir together the remaining ½ cup (4 oz/125 g) sugar and the cinnamon. Drop the dough by rounded tablespoons into the cinnamon-sugar mixture and roll to coat. Place on the prepared baking sheet, spacing the cookies about 3 inches (7.5 cm) apart. Flatten each ball slightly with the palm of your hand.

5 Bake until the cookies are golden brown on the edges but are still slightly soft in the center, 15–18 minutes. Transfer the baking sheet to a wire rack and let the cookies cool on the sheet for 5–10 minutes, then transfer the cookies to the rack and let cool completely.

TIP *Shortening is the key to the snickerdoodle's signature chewy texture, but you can swap it out for an additional ½ cup (4 oz/125 g) butter and your cookies will still be delicious.*

Variation | **Chai-Spiced Snickerdoodles**

Make the cookie dough as directed, but for the coating, replace the ¼ cup (1 oz/30 g) cinnamon with 1 tablespoon *each* ground cinnamon and ground cardamom, 2 teaspoons ground ginger, and ½ teaspoon *each* ground cloves and freshly ground pepper. Stir this spice mixture into the ½ cup (4 oz/125 g) sugar and coat as directed.

Chocolate Crinkle Cookies

With their craggy tops and soft, chewy interiors, these cookies are crowd-pleasers. To boost the chocolate factor, roll the dough balls in equal parts confectioners' sugar and cocoa powder. Using room-temperature ingredients ensures that the dough comes together evenly and that the cookies all have the same texture.

1⅔ cups (8 ½ oz/265 g)
all-purpose flour

½ cup (1½ oz/45 g) plus 1 tablespoon
unsweetened cocoa powder
or Dutch-process cocoa powder

1½ teaspoons baking powder

¼ teaspoon kosher salt

½ cup (4 oz/125 g) unsalted butter,
at room temperature

1¼ cups (10 oz/315 g) granulated
sugar

2 large eggs

½ teaspoon pure vanilla extract

½ cup (2 oz/60 g) confectioners'
sugar

Makes about 18 cookies

1 Preheat the oven to 350°F (180°C). Line a baking sheet with parchment paper.

2 In a bowl, sift together the flour, cocoa powder, baking powder, and salt. Set aside.

3 In the bowl of a stand mixer fitted with the paddle attachment, beat together the butter and granulated sugar on medium speed until light and fluffy, about 3 minutes. Reduce the speed to low and add the eggs one at a time, beating well after each addition. Add the vanilla and beat until combined, about 1 minute. Stop the mixer and scrape down the sides of the bowl. Add the flour mixture and beat on low speed until combined, about 1 minute.

4 Place the confectioners' sugar in a small bowl. Scoop up a rounded tablespoon of the dough and roll between your palms into a ball. Roll the ball in the confectioners' sugar and place on the prepared baking sheet. Repeat with the remaining dough, spacing the cookies about 2 inches (5 cm) apart. Flatten each ball slightly with the palm of your hand.

5 Bake until the cookies are crackled and puffed, 10–12 minutes. Transfer the baking sheet to a wire rack and let the cookies cool on the sheet for 3 minutes, then transfer the cookies to the rack and let cool slightly before serving.

Chocolate-Dipped Coconut Macaroons

An ideal gluten-free treat, these macaroons are also a welcome sight for anyone who craves coconut and chocolate. For a more intense flavor, spread the coconut on a baking sheet and toast in the preheated oven just until it begins to color, 6–8 minutes. Let cool before mixing with the other ingredients.

3½ cups (14 oz/440 g) shredded dried sweetened coconut

¾ cup (6 oz/185 g) sugar

5 large egg whites, lightly beaten

1½ teaspoons pure vanilla extract

¼ teaspoon almond extract

¾ lb (375 g) bittersweet or semisweet chocolate, finely chopped

Makes about 18 macaroons

1 Line a baking sheet with parchment paper. In a bowl, combine the coconut, sugar, egg whites, and vanilla and almond extracts and stir well. Spread on the prepared baking sheet and refrigerate until cold, about 30 minutes.

2 Preheat the oven to 300°F (150°C). Line another baking sheet with parchment paper.

3 Scoop up the coconut mixture by heaping tablespoonfuls and pack into small, rounded domes. Place on the prepared baking sheet.

4 Bake until the macaroons are golden, about 30 minutes. Transfer the macaroons to a wire rack and let cool completely. Line the baking sheet with a fresh sheet of parchment paper.

5 Place the chocolate in a heatproof bowl set over (but not touching) barely simmering water in a saucepan and heat, stirring often, until melted and smooth. Remove the bowl from over the water. Dip the bottom of each macaroon in the melted chocolate to a depth of about ¼ inch (6 mm). Place, chocolate side down, on the prepared baking sheet. Refrigerate until the chocolate is firm, about 1 hour.

TIP *These macaroons are great make-ahead cookies. Refrigerate them in an airtight container for up to 3 days. Let stand at room temperature for about 1 hour before serving.*

Perfect Chocolate Chip Cookies

Choose a high-quality flaky sea salt, such as Maldon or fleur de sel, for topping these iconic cookies. The salt deepens the chocolate flavor and tempers the sweetness. If you like, stir in 1 cup (4 oz/125 g) pecans or walnuts, toasted and coarsely chopped, with the chocolate chunks.

2¼ cups (11½ oz/360 g) all-purpose flour

1 teaspoon baking soda

1 teaspoon kosher salt

1 cup (8 oz/250 g) unsalted butter, at room temperature

⅔ cup (5 oz/155 g) granulated sugar

⅔ cup (5 oz/155 g) firmly packed light brown sugar

1 large egg plus 2 large egg yolks, at room temperature

2 teaspoons pure vanilla extract

¾ lb (375 g) semisweet chocolate, cut into ½-inch (12-mm) chunks

Flaky sea salt, for sprinkling

Makes about 3 dozen cookies

1 Preheat the oven to 350°F (180°C). Line a baking sheet with parchment paper.

2 In a bowl, sift together the flour, baking soda, and salt. Set aside.

3 In the bowl of a stand mixer fitted with the paddle attachment, beat together the butter, granulated sugar, and brown sugar on medium speed until light and fluffy, about 3 minutes. Reduce the speed to low, add the egg, egg yolks, and vanilla, and beat until combined, about 1 minute. Stop the mixer and scrape down the sides of the bowl. Add the flour mixture and beat on low speed until combined, about 1 minute. Stop the mixer and stir in the chocolate, distributing the chunks evenly throughout the dough.

4 Drop the dough by rounded tablespoons onto the prepared baking sheet, spacing the cookies about 1 inch (2.5 cm) apart. Sprinkle the top of the cookies with sea salt.

5 Bake until the cookies are golden brown, 8–10 minutes. Transfer the baking sheet to a wire rack and let the cookies cool on the sheet for 3 minutes, then transfer the cookies to the rack and let cool slightly before serving.

Cookie dough freezes well. Form into balls or rounded tablespoon shapes and freeze, wrapped in plastic wrap or placed in a zippered plastic bag. There's no need to thaw the dough; bake as many cookies as you want and increase the cooking time by 1 to 2 minutes.

Variation | **Salted-Caramel Chocolate Chip Cookies**

Make the cookie dough as directed and scoop into 1½-tablespoon rounds. Cut 12 salted caramel candies in half. Press a caramel half into the center of each round and press the dough together to completely enclose the caramel. Roll into a ball and bake as directed, increasing the baking time to 10–12 minutes.

SANDWICH COOKIES & BARS

Homemade Oreos

Here, Oreos, the best-selling cookie in the United States for more than a century, are re-created in the home kitchen. If you don't have a piping bag, fill a plastic bag half full with the filling. Twist the top closed and snip off about ¼ inch (6 mm) from a bottom corner.

FOR THE COOKIES

1¼ cups (6½ oz/200 g) all-purpose flour, plus more for dusting

¾ cup (6 oz/185 g) granulated sugar

¾ cup (2¼ oz/65 g) unsweetened Dutch-process cocoa powder

1 teaspoon baking soda

¼ teaspoon baking powder

¼ teaspoon kosher salt

¾ cup (6 oz/185 g) unsalted butter, at room temperature

1 large egg plus 1 large egg yolk

FOR THE FILLING

½ cup (4 oz/125 g) unsalted butter, at room temperature

1½ cups (6 oz/185 g) confectioners' sugar

1 tablespoon whole milk

1 teaspoon pure vanilla extract

Makes about 1 dozen sandwich cookies

1 To make the cookies, preheat the oven to 375°F (190°C). Line a baking sheet with parchment paper.

2 In the bowl of a stand mixer fitted with the whisk attachment, whisk together the flour, granulated sugar, cocoa powder, baking soda, baking powder, and salt. Fit the mixer with the paddle attachment, add the butter, and beat on low speed until incorporated, about 2 minutes, then beat in the egg and egg yolk. Raise the speed to medium and beat until the dough comes together, about 2 minutes.

3 Turn the dough out onto a well-floured surface and roll out ¼ inch (6 mm) thick. Using a 2-inch (5-cm) round cutter, cut out cookies. Transfer the cookies to the prepared baking sheet, spacing them about 2 inches (5 cm) apart. Gather up the scraps of dough, reroll, and cut out more cookies, refrigerating the dough for 15 minutes if it gets too warm.

4 Bake until the cookies are firm to the touch, 8–10 minutes. Transfer the baking sheet to a wire rack and let the cookies cool on the sheet for 5 minutes, then transfer the cookies to the rack and let cool completely.

5 Meanwhile, make the filling: In the clean bowl of the stand mixer fitted with the clean paddle attachment, beat together the butter, confectioners' sugar, milk, and vanilla on medium-high speed until smooth and well combined, about 3 minutes. Transfer to a pastry bag fitted with a ½-inch (12-mm) tip.

6 Pipe a layer of the filling (about 2 teaspoons) on the flat side of half of the cookies. Top with the remaining cookies, flat side down, and gently press together.

TIP *To give your Oreos a mint flavor, add 1 teaspoon peppermint extract with the egg and egg yolk.*

Linzer Cookies

These crumbly, buttery, jam-packed cookies are named for the Austrian city of Linz. They can be sandwiched with nearly any jam, including raspberry, apricot, blackberry, strawberry, or black currant. For a pretty presentation, use a small decorative cutter—a star, heart, or diamond, for example—to cut the window in each top cookie.

1 cup (5 oz/155 g) hazelnuts, toasted and skinned, or slivered almonds, toasted

½ cup (4 oz/125 g) unsalted butter, at room temperature

½ cup (4 oz/125 g) granulated sugar

1 large egg yolk

1 teaspoon finely grated orange or lemon zest

¾ teaspoon pure vanilla extract

¼ teaspoon almond extract

1 cup (5 oz/155 g) all-purpose flour

½ teaspoon ground cinnamon

¼ teaspoon kosher salt

About ¼ cup (2½ oz/75 g) seedless raspberry jam

Confectioners' sugar, for dusting

Makes about 18 sandwich cookies

1 In a food processor, finely grind the hazelnuts using short pulses. Set aside. In a large bowl, using an electric mixer on high speed, cream the butter until fluffy and pale yellow. Add the granulated sugar and continue beating until combined. Add the egg yolk, orange zest, vanilla, and almond extract and beat on low speed until well blended.

2 Sift the flour, cinnamon, and salt together into another bowl. Add the ground hazelnuts and stir to blend. Add the flour-nut mixture to the butter mixture and mix on low speed or stir with a wooden spoon until blended. The dough should be soft. Turn the dough out, divide into 4 equal pieces, and wrap each in plastic wrap. Refrigerate until chilled, about 1 hour.

3 Preheat the oven to 350°F (180°C). Line 2 baking sheets with parchment paper. Remove 1 piece of the dough at a time from the refrigerator, place between 2 sheets of waxed paper, and roll out ¼ inch (6 mm) thick. Using a cookie cutter about 2½ inches (6 cm) in diameter, cut out the cookies. Repeat to roll out the remaining dough portions, then reroll the dough scraps to make 36 cookies total. If the dough becomes sticky, wrap it in plastic wrap and chill in the freezer for about 10 minutes before rolling out. Cut a hole in the center of 18 of the cookies using a 1¼-inch (3-cm) cutter.

4 Using a thin spatula, carefully transfer the cookies to the prepared baking sheets. Bake until firm to the touch, about 12 minutes. Transfer the baking sheets to wire racks. Loosen the cookies from the baking sheets with the spatula, but let the cookies cool on the sheets.

5 To assemble, spread the solid cookies with about 1 teaspoon of the raspberry jam, leaving a ¼-inch (6-mm) border. Top the solid cookies with the cutout cookies, pressing them together gently. Using a fine-mesh sieve, dust the cookies with confectioners' sugar.

TIP *Metal cookie cutters give the cutout dough shapes cleaner, more defined edges than plastic cookie cutters.*

Chocolate Pretzel–Peanut Butter Sandwich Cookies

Chocolate and peanut butter make an unbeatable combination, and the addition of salty pretzels only heightens the appeal. If using natural peanut butter, made without the additives that prevent the oil from separating, stir in the oil layer thoroughly before measuring. Cashew or almond butter is a good choice for anyone with a peanut allergy.

1 recipe Shortbread Cookies
(page 75)

FOR THE FILLING

½ cup (4 oz/125 g) unsalted butter,
at room temperature

1 cup (10 oz/315 g) creamy peanut
butter

1½ cups (6 oz/185 g) confectioners'
sugar

Pinch of kosher salt

6 tablespoons (90 ml) whole milk

**FOR THE CHOCOLATE-PRETZEL
TOPPING**

2 cups (12 oz/375 g) dark
or semisweet chocolate chips

1½ cups (3 oz/90 g) mini pretzels,
crushed

*Makes about 18
sandwich cookies*

1 Make the cookie dough, following the directions for cutting them into triangles, and bake. Let cool completely.

2 Meanwhile, make the filling: In the bowl of a stand mixer fitted with the paddle attachment, beat together the butter and peanut butter on medium-high speed until well combined, about 1 minute. Reduce the speed to low, slowly add the confectioners' sugar and salt, and beat until combined, about 1 minute. Add the milk, 1 tablespoon at a time, and beat until completely incorporated. Raise the speed to high and beat until light and fluffy, about 3 minutes.

3 Line a baking sheet with parchment paper and put half of the cookies on the prepared baking sheet. Spread 2 teaspoons of filling in an even layer onto the flat side of each cookie. Top with the remaining cookies, flat side down, and gently press together. Freeze until the filling is firm and the cookies are cold, about 10 minutes.

4 Meanwhile, line a second baking sheet with parchment paper. Place the chocolate chips in a heatproof bowl set over (but not touching) barely simmering water in a saucepan and heat, stirring often, until melted and smooth. Working in batches to ensure the cookies stay cold, dip each frozen sandwich cookie halfway into the melted chocolate and immediately sprinkle crushed pretzels over the chocolate, gently pressing them into the chocolate. Carefully place on the prepared baking sheet and let stand at room temperature until the chocolate is set.

TIP *To crush the pretzels, put them in a small food processor and pulse until finely chopped. Or, place the pretzels in a zippered plastic bag, seal it, and gently hit it with a rolling pin to break them up.*

Lemon Cream Sandwich Cookies

For a fancier finish, skip the dusting of confectioners' sugar. Instead, melt ¾ cup (4½ oz/140 g) white chocolate chips in a bowl over (but not touching) barely simmering water in a saucepan, stirring until smooth. Dip half of each cookie in the chocolate and then in a bowl of finely chopped toasted nuts of choice. Place on parchment or waxed paper until the chocolate sets.

FOR THE COOKIES

2 cups (10 oz/315 g) all-purpose flour, plus more as needed

½ teaspoon baking powder

¼ teaspoon kosher salt

¾ cup (6 oz/185 g) unsalted butter, at room temperature

½ cup (4 oz/125 g) granulated sugar

3 large egg yolks

1 teaspoon pure vanilla extract

2 teaspoons grated lemon zest

2 tablespoons fresh lemon juice

FOR THE FILLING

¼ lb (125 g) cream cheese, at room temperature

4 tablespoons (2 oz/60 g) unsalted butter, at room temperature

1½ teaspoons grated lemon zest

3 tablespoons fresh lemon juice

½ cup (2 oz/60 g) confectioners' sugar, plus more for dusting

¼ teaspoon kosher salt

Makes about 2 dozen sandwich cookies

1 To make the cookies, in a bowl, sift together the flour, baking powder, and salt. Set aside.

2 In the bowl of a stand mixer fitted with the paddle attachment, beat together the butter and granulated sugar on medium speed until light and fluffy, about 3 minutes. Reduce the speed to low, add the egg yolks, vanilla, and lemon zest and juice and beat until combined, about 1 minute. Stop the mixer and scrape down the sides of the bowl. Add the flour mixture and beat on low speed until combined, about 1 minute. If the dough is still sticky, beat in more flour, 1–2 tablespoons at a time, until it is no longer sticky. Turn the dough out onto a work surface, divide into 2 equal pieces, and shape each into a disk. Wrap separately in plastic wrap and refrigerate for at least 30 minutes or up to overnight. Let the dough soften slightly at room temperature before continuing.

3 Preheat the oven to 350°F (180°C). Line a baking sheet with parchment paper.

4 On a lightly floured work surface, roll out 1 dough disk ⅛ inch (3 mm) thick. Using a 2-inch (5-cm) round cutter, cut out cookies. Transfer the cookies to the prepared baking sheet, spacing them about 2 inches (5 cm) apart. Repeat with the remaining dough disk.

5 Bake until the cookies are firm to the touch and the edges are golden brown, 10–11 minutes. Transfer to a wire rack and let cool completely.

6 Meanwhile, make the filling: In the clean bowl of the stand mixer fitted with a clean paddle attachment, beat together the cream cheese, butter, lemon zest and juice, confectioners' sugar, and salt on high speed until fluffy, about 3 minutes.

7 Spread about 1 tablespoon of the filling on the flat side of half of the cookies. Top with the remaining cookies, flat side down, and gently press together. Just before serving, dust the cookies with confectioners' sugar.

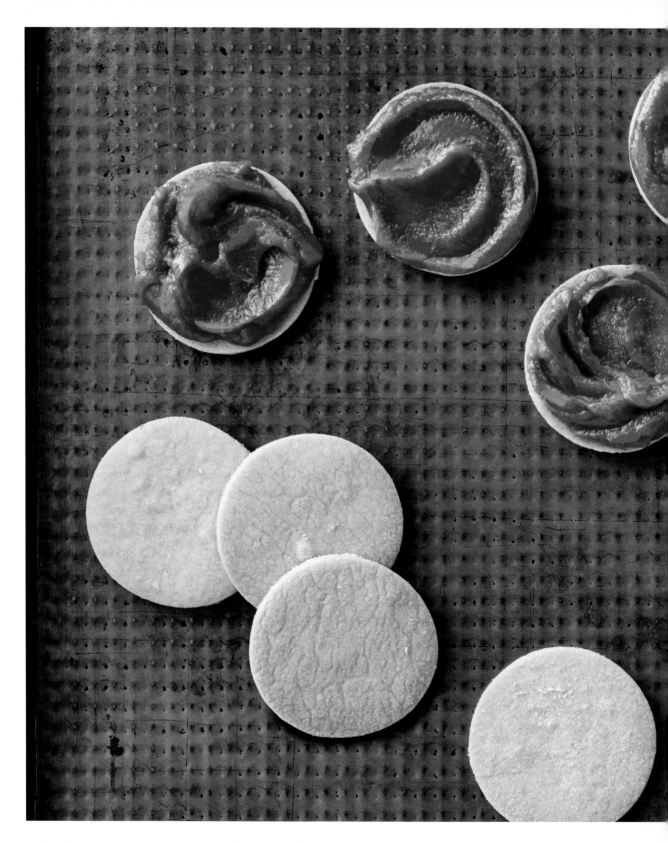

c Alfajores

...lar sweets traveled from North Africa to Spain to South America, where they changed from nutty finger-shaped cookies into shortbread-like sandwich cookies, usually bound together with the creamy caramel concoction known as dulce de leche. If you favor citrus flavors, add 2 teaspoons grated lemon zest and ½ teaspoon lemon extract with the vanilla and egg yolks.

2 cups (10 oz/315 g) all-purpose flour, plus more for dusting

2 tablespoons cornstarch

½ teaspoon kosher salt

¾ cup (6 oz/185 g) cold unsalted butter, cut into cubes

½ cup (2 oz/60 g) confectioners' sugar

2 teaspoons pure vanilla extract

2 large egg yolks

1 can (13 oz/410 g) dulce de leche

Makes about 1 dozen sandwich cookies

1 Preheat the oven to 325°F (165°C). Line a baking sheet with parchment paper.

2 In a food processor, combine the flour, cornstarch, and salt and pulse until blended. Add the butter and pulse until the texture resembles fine crumbs. Add the confectioners' sugar, vanilla, and egg yolks and process until the dough comes together in a single mass.

3 Turn the dough out onto a well-floured surface and roll out ¼ inch (6 mm) thick. Using a 2-inch (5-cm) round cutter, cut out cookies. Transfer the cookies to the prepared baking sheet, spacing them about 1½ inches (4 cm) apart. Gather up the scraps of dough, reroll, and cut out more cookies, refrigerating the dough for 15 minutes if it gets too warm.

4 Bake until the cookies are lightly golden brown on the edges, 13–15 minutes. Transfer the baking sheet to a wire rack and let cool completely.

5 Spread about 1 tablespoon of the dulce de leche on the flat side of half of the cookies. Top with the remaining cookies, flat side down, and gently press together.

TIP *Dust the alfajores with confectioners' sugar, sprinkle finely shredded coconut around the edge of the filling, or dip the cookies in melted chocolate.*

Alfajores with Buttered Rum & Vanilla Bean Filling

Alfajores are made in many countries with countless variations. Traditionally filled with dulce de leche, the cookies can also be filled with jams or other fillings. This yummy variation of the classic version features a rum-flavored filling—perfect for rum lovers. Save your fresh vanilla pod for future baking recipes, or make vanilla sugar by placing it in a jar of granulated sugar.

2 cups (14 oz/440 g) firmly packed light brown sugar

1 cup (250 ml) heavy cream

4 tablespoons (2 oz/60 g) unsalted butter

½ teaspoon kosher salt

3 tablespoons aged rum

1 vanilla bean, split, with seeds scraped and reserved

1 recipe Classic Alfajores (facing page)

Makes about 1 dozen sandwich cookies

1 In a saucepan over medium heat, combine the brown sugar, cream, butter, and salt. Cook, stirring frequently, until the mixture begins to simmer, about 3 minutes. Reduce the heat to medium-low and cook, stirring frequently, until thickened, about 15 minutes. Remove from the heat, stir in the rum and vanilla bean seeds, and transfer to a bowl. Let cool to room temperature, then cover and refrigerate until firm, about 1 hour.

2 Make the cookie dough and bake as directed, filling the cookies with the buttered rum filling instead of the dulce de leche.

TIP *To scrape out the seeds of a vanilla bean, use a small knife to cut the bean in half lengthwise. Use the back of the knife to scrape out the seeds from the inside of the pod. If you don't have a vanilla bean, substitute 1 tablespoon of pure vanilla extract instead.*

Crunchy Toffee Triangles

The buttery toffee bits give these chewy, moist bar cookies a delicious crunch. Almonds are the most common partner for toffee—think Heath bars—but pecans or walnuts work well here, too. To end up with uniform triangles, cut the baked dessert into 3-by-4-inch (7.5-by-10-cm) rectangles (use a ruler for accuracy), then cut each rectangle in half diagonally.

1 cup (8 oz/250 g) unsalted butter, at room temperature, plus more for greasing

2¼ cups (11½ oz/360 g) all-purpose flour

1 teaspoon baking powder

¼ teaspoon kosher salt

1 cup (8 oz/250 g) granulated sugar

1 cup (7 oz/220 g) firmly packed dark brown sugar

2 large eggs

1 teaspoon pure vanilla extract

½ lb (250 g) toffee pieces

¾ cup (3 oz/90 g) whole almonds, lightly toasted and coarsely chopped

Makes 18 triangles

1 Preheat the oven to 350°F (180°C). Butter a 9-by-13-inch (23-by-33-cm) baking dish. Line with parchment paper, letting the paper overhang on the long sides by 1 inch (2.5 cm).

2 In a bowl, sift together the flour, baking powder, and salt. Set aside.

3 In the bowl of a stand mixer fitted with the paddle attachment, beat together the butter, granulated sugar, and brown sugar on medium speed until light and fluffy, about 3 minutes. Reduce the speed to low, and add the eggs one at a time, beating well after each addition. Add the vanilla and beat until combined. Stop the mixer and scrape down the sides of the bowl. Slowly add the flour mixture and beat on low speed until almost incorporated. Add the toffee pieces and beat until just incorporated.

4 Spread the dough evenly in the prepared baking dish and sprinkle the top evenly with the almonds.

5 Bake until golden around the edges and a toothpick inserted into the center comes out with only moist crumbs attached, about 25 minutes. Transfer the baking dish to a wire rack and let cool completely, about 1 hour. Run a metal spatula around the edges of the dish and use the parchment paper to lift the dessert from the dish. Cut into 18 triangles and serve.

TIP *If you can't find toffee bits or you crave a chocolaty twist, substitute an 8-oz (250-g) milk chocolate bar, chopped into small pieces, for the toffee.*

Seven-Layer Bars

You won't need a mixing bowl and spoon to make these buttery, nutty, chocolaty bars. Just layer the ingredients in the dish and bake. If you like, trade out half of the bittersweet chocolate chips for white chocolate chips, or substitute peanut butter chips for the butterscotch chips.

½ cup (4 oz/125 g) unsalted butter

1½ cups (4½ oz/140 g) graham cracker crumbs (about 10 crackers)

1½ cups (9 oz/280 g) bittersweet chocolate chips

1 cup (6 oz/185 g) butterscotch chips

1 cup (3 oz/90 g) rolled oats

1 cup (4 oz/125 g) pecans, toasted and chopped

1 cup (4 oz/125 g) walnuts, toasted and chopped

1 can (14 fl oz/430 ml) sweetened condensed milk

1½ cups (6 oz/185 g) shredded dried unsweetened coconut

Makes 20 bars

1 Preheat the oven to 350°F (180°C).

2 Put the butter in a 9-by-13-inch (23-by-33-cm) baking dish and transfer to the oven. When the butter has melted, swirl to coat the bottom and sides of the dish.

3 Spread the graham cracker crumbs in an even layer on the bottom of the dish. Layer the chocolate chips, butterscotch chips, oats, pecans, and walnuts on top. Pour the condensed milk over the entire surface. Sprinkle the coconut on top.

4 Bake until the coconut is toasted and the edges are golden brown, 20–25 minutes. Transfer the baking dish to a wire rack and let cool completely, then cut into bars.

To crush the graham crackers, put them in a small food processor and pulse until finely chopped. Or, place them in a zippered plastic bag, seal it, and gently hit it with a rolling pin to break them up.

Lemon Bars

These sweet-tart bars are guaranteed to disappear quickly at any gathering. Take the time to refrigerate the crust before baking to ensure it will crisp and brown in the oven. For a hint of lemon flavor in the crust, add 1 teaspoon grated lemon zest with the flour and sugar.

FOR THE CRUST

1¼ cups (6½ oz/200 g) all-purpose flour

½ cup (2 oz/60 g) confectioners' sugar

¼ cup (1 oz/30 g) cornstarch

½ teaspoon kosher salt

½ cup (4 oz/125 g) plus 3 tablespoons cold unsalted butter, cut into ½-inch (12-mm) pieces

1 tablespoon cold water

FOR THE FILLING

3 large eggs plus 3 large egg yolks

1 cup (8 oz/250 g) granulated sugar

3 tablespoons all-purpose flour

½ teaspoon kosher salt

3 teaspoons grated lemon zest

¾ cup (180 ml) fresh lemon juice

⅓ cup (80 ml) whole milk

Confectioners' sugar, for dusting

Makes 16 bars

1 To make the crust, preheat the oven to 350°F (180°C). Lightly grease an 8-inch (20-cm) square baking dish. Line with parchment paper, letting the paper overhang on two opposite sides by 2 inches (5 cm).

2 In a food processor, combine the flour, confectioners' sugar, cornstarch, and salt and pulse until blended. Add the butter and pulse until the mixture is coarse and pale yellow, 8–10 pulses. Add the cold water and pulse until just combined, 2–4 pulses.

3 Sprinkle the mixture into the prepared dish and press firmly into an even layer ¼–½ inch (6–12 mm) thick over the bottom of the dish and about ½ inch (12 mm) up the sides. Refrigerate for 20 minutes.

4 Bake until the crust is golden brown, 25–30 minutes. Reduce the oven temperature to 325°F (165°C).

5 To make the filling, in a bowl, whisk together the eggs, egg yolks, granulated sugar, flour, salt, lemon zest and juice, and milk until combined. Pour the filling on top of the warm crust.

6 Bake until the filling is just set and barely jiggles in the center, 25–30 minutes. Transfer the baking dish to a wire rack and let cool for about 30 minutes. Use the parchment paper to lift the dessert from the dish. Cut into 16 bars and dust generously with confectioners' sugar.

TIP *An excellent make-ahead dessert for parties, these lemon bars set up more if you chill them. Cover the dish with plastic wrap and refrigerate for up to 3 days before cutting into bars.*

Variation | **Orange Creamsicle Bars**

Make and bake the crust as directed. Make the filling, replacing the lemon zest, lemon juice, and milk with 5 teaspoons grated orange zest, 3 teaspoons grated lemon zest, ¾ cup (180 ml) fresh orange juice, ⅓ cup (80 ml) heavy cream, and 1 teaspoon orange-flower water (optional). Pour the filling on top of the warm crust and bake as directed.

Peanut Butter–Crispy Rice Brownies

*These showy bar cookies will please children and grown-ups alike. What's not to love?
A brownie topped with velvety ganache; a gooey, crunchy mix of peanut butter, marshmallows,
and crisped rice cereal; and a second layer of ganache. The key to easy layering is making sure
that each component of this dessert is completely cooled before assembling the layers.*

FOR THE BROWNIES

½ cup (4 oz/125 g) unsalted butter,
cut into 4 pieces, plus more for
greasing

3 oz (90 g) unsweetened chocolate,
finely chopped

1 cup (8 oz/250 g) sugar

Pinch of kosher salt

2 large eggs, at room temperature

1 teaspoon pure vanilla extract

¾ cup (4 oz/125 g) all-purpose flour

¾ cup (4½ oz/140 g) bittersweet
chocolate chips

FOR THE GANACHE

½ lb (250 g) semisweet or
bittersweet chocolate chips

1 cup (250 ml) heavy cream

Pinch of kosher salt

FOR THE PEANUT BUTTER–
CRISPY RICE

5 tablespoons (2½ oz/75 g)
unsalted butter

5 cups (8¾ oz/270 g) mini
marshmallows

½ cup (5 oz/155 g) creamy peanut
butter

5 cups (5 oz/140 g) crisp rice cereal

Makes 16 bars

1 To make the brownies, preheat the oven to 350°F (180°C). Lightly grease an 8-inch (20-cm) square baking dish. Line the dish with parchment paper, letting the paper overhang on two opposite sides by about 2 inches (5 cm), and lightly grease the parchment.

2 In a large microwave-safe bowl, melt the butter and chocolate in the microwave in 30-second increments, whisking occasionally. When melted, whisk in the sugar and salt. Add the eggs and vanilla and whisk until combined. Gently fold in the flour and chocolate chips.

3 Pour the batter into the prepared dish and spread evenly. Bake until a toothpick inserted into the center of the brownies comes out almost completely clean, about 30 minutes. Transfer the dish to a wire rack and let cool completely.

4 To make the ganache, put the chocolate chips in a heatproof bowl. In a saucepan over medium-high heat, bring the cream to a boil. Pour over the chocolate chips and add the salt. Let stand for 10 minutes, then whisk until smooth and shiny. Refrigerate until chilled but not hardened, about 20 minutes. Set aside ¼ cup (60 ml) of the ganache. Pour the remaining ganache over the brownies and spread evenly, then refrigerate while making the peanut butter–crispy rice.

5 To make the peanut butter–crispy rice, in a large saucepan over low heat, melt the butter. Add the marshmallows and stir until melted. Remove from the heat and stir in the peanut butter until completely incorporated. Add the crisp rice cereal and stir until well coated. Let cool completely, then gently press the mixture evenly over the chilled ganache layer. Using a piping bag fitted with a ¼-inch tip, drizzle the reserved ganache over the surface. Use the parchment paper to lift the dessert from the dish. Cut into 16 bars.

Classic Dark Chocolate Brownies

Sometimes a classic is just what you want and in the case of brownies, these fudgy, rich squares fit the bill. But this recipe can also be easily embellished. Crave a double dose of chocolate? Stir ½ cup (3 oz/90 g) semisweet, milk, or white chocolate chips into the batter before baking. Or try adding 1 teaspoon peppermint extract to the batter for a minty twist.

¾ cup (6 oz/185 g) unsalted butter, cut into ¾-inch (2-cm) pieces, plus more for greasing

6 ounces (125 g) unsweetened chocolate, chopped

3 large eggs

1¾ cups (14 oz/440 g) sugar

¼ teaspoon kosher salt

2 teaspoons pure vanilla extract

1 cup (5 oz/155 g) all-purpose flour

Makes 16 brownies

1 Position a rack in the middle of the oven and preheat to 350°F (180°C). Butter an 8-inch (20-cm) square baking dish.

2 Place the chocolate and butter in a large heatproof bowl set over (but not touching) barely simmering water in a saucepan. Heat, stirring often, until the butter and chocolate melt. Remove from over the water and let cool slightly.

3 In a large bowl, whisk together the eggs, sugar, salt, and vanilla until blended. Whisk in the chocolate mixture until blended. Sprinkle the flour over the mixture and whisk slowly just until blended. Pour the batter into the prepared dish, spreading it evenly with a rubber spatula.

4 Bake until a toothpick inserted into the center comes out almost clean or with a few moist crumbs attached, 35–40 minutes. Be careful not to overbake. Transfer the dish to a wire rack and let cool completely.

5 Using a large, sharp knife, cut into 2-inch (5-cm) squares.

If a few moist crumbs cling to the toothpick, it is time to remove the dish from the oven. If you're in doubt, run your fingers over the toothpick. If the toothpick feels wet, it has moist batter on it, which means the brownies need more time in the oven.

White Chocolate Chip Blondies

This butterscotch-flavored bar cookie is a welcome addition to school lunch boxes, afternoon teas, and picnic baskets. If you're feeling indulgent, treat these bars to a caramel glaze: combine ½ lb (250 g) high-quality caramel candies and ¼ cup (60 ml) water in a saucepan over low heat, stirring until smooth, then drizzle over the cut bars.

¾ cup (6 oz/185 g) unsalted butter, at room temperature, plus more for greasing

1¼ cups (6 ½ oz/200 g) all-purpose flour

1 teaspoon baking powder

¼ teaspoon kosher salt

1 cup (7 oz/220 g) firmly packed light brown sugar

1 teaspoon pure vanilla extract

2 large eggs

¼ cup (1½ oz/45 g) white chocolate chips

Makes 12–16 bars

1 Preheat the oven to 350°F (180°C). Butter an 8-inch (20-cm) square baking dish.

2 In a bowl, sift together the flour, baking powder, and salt. Set aside.

3 In the bowl of a stand mixer fitted with the paddle attachment, beat together the butter, brown sugar, and vanilla on medium speed until light and fluffy, about 3 minutes. Reduce the speed to low and add the eggs one at a time, beating well after each addition. Raise the speed to medium-high and beat until very fluffy, about 2 minutes. Stop the mixer and scrape down the sides of the bowl. Add the flour mixture and beat on low speed until combined, about 1 minute. Stop the mixer and fold in the white chocolate chips until just blended.

4 Scrape the batter into the prepared dish and spread evenly.

5 Bake until a toothpick inserted into the center comes out clean, 25–30 minutes. Transfer the dish to a wire rack and let cool completely. Cut into bars and serve.

Variation | **Brown Butter & Hazelnut Blondies**

In a large sauté pan over medium heat, melt 1 cup (8 oz/250 g) unsalted butter. Reduce the heat to medium-low and simmer gently, swirling the pan often, until the butter is toasty brown and smells nutty, 5–7 minutes. Watch carefully at the end to prevent the butter from burning. Transfer to a bowl and let cool to room temperature. Refrigerate until it is the consistency of softened butter, about 30 minutes. Make the blondie batter as directed, replacing the ¾ cup (6 oz/185 g) butter with the brown butter. Fold in ⅔ cup (3¼ oz/100 g) hazelnuts, roughly chopped, with the white chocolate chips and bake as directed.

S'Mores Brownies

Anyone who lines up for both s'mores and brownies is guaranteed to swoon over these marshmallow-topped graham-cracker-laced brownies. They taste best the day they are baked, but will keep tightly covered at room temperature for up to 3 days. To pack these treats for picnics and potlucks, wrap them individually in aluminum foil or waxed paper.

1 cup (8 oz/250 g) unsalted butter, plus more for greasing

10 oz (315 g) bittersweet chocolate, finely chopped

1 cup (8 oz/250 g) granulated sugar

¾ cup (6 oz/185 g) firmly packed light brown sugar

4 large eggs

2 teaspoons pure vanilla extract

1 teaspoon kosher salt

1⅓ cups (5½ oz/170 g) cake flour

3 tablespoons natural cocoa powder

About 6 graham crackers, roughly crushed with your hands

About 12 jumbo marshmallows

Makes 12 brownies

1 Preheat the oven to 350°F (180°C). Generously butter a 9-by-13-inch (23-by-33-cm) baking dish.

2 In a large saucepan over low heat, combine the butter and chocolate and heat, stirring often, until melted, about 4 minutes. Remove from the heat and whisk in the granulated sugar and brown sugar. Whisk in the eggs one at a time, beating well after each addition. Whisk in the vanilla and salt.

3 Sift the flour and cocoa powder over the chocolate mixture and, using a rubber spatula, stir in until just blended. Stir in the graham crackers.

4 Pour the batter into the prepared baking dish and spread evenly. Top evenly with the marshmallows.

5 Bake until a toothpick inserted into the center comes out almost completely clean, 30–35 minutes. Transfer the dish to a wire rack and let cool completely. Cut into big, gooey squares.

To make it easier to cut the brownies, fill a tall glass or pitcher with very hot water. Dip your knife in the water and wipe it off with a paper towel before each cut. This technique also works great for cutting cookie bars and frosted layer cakes.

HOLIDAY COOKIES

Candy Cane Cookies

These whimsical cookies are easy to shape if you refrigerate the dough overnight as directed. If you would like less peppermint flavor, substitute ½ teaspoon pure vanilla extract for half of the peppermint extract. For a decorative finish, stir together about 1½ tablespoons each finely crushed peppermint candy and sugar and sprinkle over the just-baked cookies.

1 recipe Sugar Cookies (page 73)

1 teaspoon peppermint extract

1 teaspoon red food coloring, plus more as needed

All-purpose flour, for dusting

Makes about 2 dozen cookies

1 Make the cookie dough. Divide the dough into 2 equal pieces. Place 1 piece in the bowl of a stand mixer fitted with the paddle attachment and mix in the peppermint extract and red food coloring until completely combined. Shape each piece into a disk, wrap separately in plastic wrap, and refrigerate overnight. Let the dough soften slightly at room temperature before continuing.

2 Preheat the oven to 350°F (180°C). Line a baking sheet with parchment paper.

3 On a lightly floured work surface, roll out each dough disk ¼ inch (6 mm) thick. Cut into strips 6 inches (15 cm) long and ¾ inch (2 cm) wide. Taking 1 red strip and 1 plain strip, pinch the ends together and gently twist the strips around each other. Pinch the other end to secure and bend one end into a hook to form a candy cane shape. Transfer to the prepared baking sheet. Repeat with the remaining dough, spacing the cookies about 1½ inches (4 cm) apart.

4 Bake until the cookies are golden on the edges, about 8 minutes. Transfer the cookies to a wire rack and let cool completely.

You can also roll each disk of dough into long, skinny ropes about ½ inch (12 mm) thick and cut into 6-inch (15-cm) lengths before twisting.

Chuck's Madeleines

In the late 1950s, Chuck Williams began importing French bakeware for Williams-Sonoma, and tinned madeleine pans were among the first items he stocked. This is his recipe for the little sponge cakes that are baked in scallop shell–shaped molds. Always butter your pan, even if it's labeled nonstick, as these delicate cookies can easily stick.

4 tablespoons (2 oz/60 g) unsalted butter, very soft, plus more for greasing

½ cup (2½ oz/75 g) all-purpose flour

½ teaspoon baking powder

1 large egg

¼ cup (2 oz/60 g) granulated sugar

2 teaspoons orange-flower water

Confectioners' sugar, for dusting

Makes 1 dozen madeleines

1 Preheat the oven to 400°F (200°C). Generously butter a 12-mold madeleine pan.

2 In a bowl, sift together the flour and baking powder. Set aside.

3 In the bowl of a stand mixer fitted with the paddle attachment, beat together the egg, granulated sugar, and orange-flower water on medium speed until combined, about 30 seconds. Raise the speed to medium-high and beat until the mixture has quadrupled in bulk and is very thick, about 10 minutes. Stop the mixer and, using a rubber spatula, carefully fold in the flour mixture and then the butter.

4 Spoon the batter into the prepared molds, filling each about three-fourths full and leaving the batter mounded in the center of the wells.

5 Bake until the madeleines are lightly browned around the edges and on the bottom, 8–10 minutes. Immediately turn the madeleines out onto a wire rack. Using a fine-mesh sieve or a sifter, dust them with confectioners' sugar. Serve warm.

TIP *For an even more delicate texture, swap some or all of the all-purpose flour for cake flour. Make sure the butter is very soft so that it folds in easily.*

Variation | **Almond Madeleines**

Replace the orange-flower water with 2 teaspoons almond extract.

Variation | **Lemon Madeleines**

Replace the orange-flower water with 2 teaspooons grated lemon zest and 1 teaspoon fresh lemon juice.

Sugar Cookies

To decorate these cookies quickly and simply, sprinkle them with colored or plain sanding sugar, pearl sugar, or turbinado sugar just before baking. Alternatively, bake and cool the cookies as directed, then brush the tops with pasteurized egg whites mixed with a little water and shower lightly with decorative sugar or colored sprinkles.

2½ cups (12½ oz/390 g) all-purpose flour, plus more for dusting

1 teaspoon baking powder

½ teaspoon kosher salt

1 cup (8 oz/250 g) unsalted butter, at room temperature

¾ cup (6 oz/185 g) sugar

3 large egg yolks

1½ teaspoons pure vanilla extract

Makes about 2 dozen cookies

1 In a bowl, sift together the flour, baking powder, and salt. Set aside.

2 In the bowl of a stand mixer fitted with the paddle attachment, beat together the butter and sugar on medium speed until light and fluffy, about 3 minutes. Reduce the speed to low and add the egg yolks one at a time, beating well after each addition. Add the vanilla and beat until combined, about 1 minute. Stop the mixer and scrape down the sides of the bowl. Add the flour mixture and beat on low speed until combined, about 1 minute.

3 Turn the dough out onto a work surface, divide into 2 equal pieces, and shape each into a disk. Wrap separately in plastic wrap and refrigerate for at least 1 hour or up to overnight. Let the dough soften slightly at room temperature before continuing.

4 Preheat the oven to 350°F (180°C). Line a baking sheet with parchment paper.

5 On a lightly floured work surface, roll out 1 dough disk ¼ inch (6 mm) thick. Using cookie cutters, cut out the desired shapes. Transfer the cookies to the prepared baking sheet, spacing them about 1½ inches (4 cm) apart. Repeat with the remaining dough disk. Gather up the scraps of dough, reroll, and cut out more cookies.

6 Bake until the cookies are golden on the edges, about 8 minutes. Transfer the cookies to a wire rack and let cool completely.

TIP *Shaping the dough into smaller, flat disks before refrigerating will help it chill faster and then soften more quickly when you're ready to roll it out.*

Lemon & Black Pepper Sugar Cookies

It wouldn't be the holidays without an assortment of sugar cookies—surprise friends and family with this riff on the classic sugar cookie. Here, the combination of lemon and black pepper adds an unexpected burst of flavor, and an elegant glaze provides an additional hit of citrus.

FOR THE COOKIES

1 recipe Sugar Cookies (page 73)

4 teaspoons grated lemon zest

4 teaspoons fresh lemon juice

2 teaspoons freshly ground pepper

FOR THE GLAZE

2 cups (8 oz/250 g) confectioners' sugar

2 tablespoons whole milk

1 tablespoon grated lemon zest

1 tablespoon fresh lemon juice

1 teaspoon freshly ground pepper, plus more to taste

Makes about 2 dozen cookies

1 Make the cookie dough as directed, replacing the vanilla extract with the lemon zest and juice and pepper. Refrigerate the dough and bake as directed, then let cool completely before glazing.

2 To make the glaze, in a bowl, combine the confectioners' sugar, milk, lemon zest, lemon juice, and pepper, adding more pepper if you like. Whisk until the mixture is thick and smooth. Using a small offset spatula, spread the glaze over the top of the cookies.

Shortbread Cookies

Scotland is the birthplace of shortbread, but nowadays, everybody everywhere is hooked on this buttery, crumbly cookie. For best results, buy the finest butter you can and make sure it is at room temperature before you begin beating to safeguard against dense, tough cookies.

2 cups (10 oz/315 g) all-purpose flour, plus more for dusting

½ teaspoon kosher salt

1 cup (8 oz/250 g) unsalted butter, at room temperature

½ cup (4 oz/125 g) sugar

2 teaspoons pure vanilla extract

Makes about 3 dozen cookies

1 In a bowl, sift together the flour and salt. Set aside.

2 In the bowl of a stand mixer fitted with the paddle attachment, beat together the butter and sugar on medium speed until light and fluffy, about 3 minutes. Reduce the speed to low, add the vanilla, and beat until combined, about 1 minute. Stop the mixer and scrape down the sides of the bowl. Add the flour mixture and beat on low speed until combined, about 1 minute.

3 Turn the dough out onto a work surface and shape into a disk. Wrap in plastic wrap and refrigerate for 30 minutes.

4 Preheat the oven to 350°F (180°C). Line a baking sheet with parchment paper.

5 On a well-floured work surface, roll out the dough ¼ inch (6 mm) thick. Using a large knife, cut into 2-inch (5-cm) squares, then cut each square in half to create triangles. Transfer the cookies to the prepared baking sheet, spacing them about 1½ inches (4 cm) apart. Bake until the cookies are just golden brown on the edges, 12–14 minutes. Transfer the cookies to a wire rack and let cool completely.

TIP *Shortbread is endlessly customizable. We love the matcha variation, or you can blend citrus zest, finely ground Earl Grey tea, or dried lavender into the dough.*

Variation | **Matcha Shortbread Cookies**

Make the cookie dough as directed, whisking ¼ cup (1 oz/32 g) matcha powder into the flour and salt mixture. Beat the flour mixture into the butter mixture, then beat in 2 teaspoons heavy cream until combined. Refrigerate the dough and bake as directed.

Peppermint Candy Cookies

Dutch-process cocoa powder gives these easy-to-make fudgy cookies a rich dark color and a deep chocolate taste. To infuse the white chocolate icing with peppermint flavor, add ½ teaspoon peppermint extract with the oil. Store these cookies between sheets of waxed or parchment paper to keep them looking their best.

FOR THE COOKIES

1¼ cups (6½ oz/200 g) all-purpose flour

¾ cup (6 oz/185 g) sugar

¾ cup (2¼ oz/65 g) Dutch-process cocoa powder

1 teaspoon baking soda

¼ teaspoon baking powder

¼ teaspoon kosher salt

¾ cup (6 oz/185 g) unsalted butter, at room temperature

1 large egg plus 1 large egg yolk

1 teaspoon peppermint extract

FOR THE ICING

2 cups (12 oz/375 g) white chocolate chips

2 tablespoons canola oil

15–20 peppermint candies, crushed (about ½ cup/85 g)

Makes about 2 dozen cookies

 For a different but still festive twist during the winter holidays, replace the peppermint candies with crushed peppermint bark.

1 Preheat the oven to 375°F (190°C). Line a baking sheet with parchment paper.

2 In the bowl of a stand mixer, using a handheld whisk, whisk together the flour, sugar, cocoa powder, baking soda, baking powder, and salt. Fit the mixer with the paddle attachment, add the butter, and beat on low speed until light and fluffy, about 3 minutes, then beat in the egg, egg yolk, and peppermint extract. Raise the speed to medium and beat until the dough comes together, about 2 minutes.

3 Drop the dough by rounded tablespoons onto the prepared baking sheet, spacing the cookies about 2 inches (5 cm) apart. Flatten each ball slightly with the palm of your hand.

4 Bake until the cookies are firm to the touch, 8–10 minutes. Transfer the baking sheet to a wire rack and let the cookies cool on the sheet for 5 minutes, then transfer the cookies to the rack and let cool completely.

5 Meanwhile, make the icing: Place the white chocolate chips in a heatproof bowl set over (but not touching) barely simmering water in a saucepan and heat, stirring occasionally, until the chocolate is melted. Remove from the heat and stir in the oil until smooth.

6 Line another baking sheet with parchment paper. Dip each cookie halfway into the melted white chocolate, then immediately sprinkle peppermint candies over the white chocolate. Place on the prepared baking sheet. If the white chocolate begins to harden, set the bowl over simmering water for up to 1 minute to remelt. Let the cookies set up for 15 minutes before serving.

Ginger-Molasses Cookies

Cookies that showcase ginger and molasses turn up everywhere, from New England to Scandinavia to the Czech Republic. This version, heady with ginger as well as cinnamon and allspice, pairs well with afternoon coffee or tea in the cool-weather months. For a bright citrus touch, mix in 2 teaspoons grated orange zest with the molasses.

2 cups (10 oz/315 g) all-purpose flour

1½ teaspoons baking soda

¼ teaspoon kosher salt

1½ teaspoons ground ginger

1 teaspoon ground cinnamon

½ teaspoon ground allspice

¾ cup (6 oz/185 g) unsalted butter, at room temperature

1 cup (7 oz/220 g) firmly packed light brown sugar

1 large egg

⅓ cup (3¾ oz/115 g) light molasses

½ cup (3½ oz/100 g) turbinado sugar

Makes about 3 dozen cookies

1 Preheat the oven to 350°F (180°C). Line a baking sheet with parchment paper.

2 In a bowl, sift together the flour, baking soda, salt, ginger, cinnamon, and allspice. Set aside.

3 In the bowl of a stand mixer fitted with the paddle attachment, beat together the butter and brown sugar on medium speed until light and fluffy, about 3 minutes. Reduce the speed to low, add the egg and molasses, and beat until combined, about 1 minute. Stop the mixer and scrape down the sides of the bowl. Add the flour mixture and beat on low speed until combined, about 1 minute.

4 Drop the dough by rounded tablespoonfuls onto the prepared baking sheet, spacing the cookies about 2 inches (5 cm) apart. Sprinkle the cookies generously with the turbinado sugar.

5 Bake until the cookies are browned and firm to the touch, 10–12 minutes. Transfer the baking sheet to a wire rack and let the cookies cool on the sheet for 5 minutes, then transfer the cookies to the rack and let cool completely.

 TIP *To add an extra kick of ginger, stir finely chopped candied ginger into the dough after beating in the flour mixture.*

Checkerboard Cookies

Although these cookies look difficult to make, they are actually quite easy, plus the dough can be mixed and layered in advance. You can refrigerate it overnight or freeze it for up to 1 month. If frozen, let stand at room temperature for a few minutes before slicing and baking.

1 recipe Chocolate Sugar Cookies (page 91)

1 recipe Sugar Cookies (page 73)

All-purpose flour, for flouring your hands

1 egg white

Makes about 30 cookies

1 Make the Chocolate Sugar Cookies dough, omitting the step where the dough is shaped into a rectangle. Instead, shape the dough into a ball, wrap in plastic wrap, and chill as directed. Make the Sugar Cookies dough, omitting the step where the dough is divided into two balls. Instead, shape the dough into 1 ball, wrap in plastic wrap, and chill as directed.

2 Remove the dough from the refrigerator. Cut each piece of dough into 6 strips. One at a time, roll each strip between your palms into a rope 7 ½ inches (19 cm) long, flouring your hands lightly, if necessary. In a small bowl, using a fork, beat the egg white until foamy. On a work surface, lay 3 ropes parallel to one another, alternating the colors—chocolate, vanilla, chocolate—and press the ropes together. Brush some of the egg white lightly on the top. Place a second set of 3 ropes of alternating colors—vanilla, chocolate, vanilla—on top of the first set, press them together, and brush with egg white. Press the layers gently to seal them together. Repeat once more, alternating the colors—chocolate, vanilla, chocolate—so that you have a stack of 3 rows and a checkerboard pattern is visible when the stack is viewed from the end. Do not brush the top row with egg white. Trim the ends evenly. Wrap in plastic wrap and refrigerate until firm, at least 1 hour or up to overnight.

3 Preheat the oven to 350°F (180°C). Line 2 baking sheets with parchment paper.

4 Unwrap the checkerboard log on a cutting board. Using a large, sharp knife, cut the dough crosswise into slices ¼ inch (6 mm) thick. Transfer the cookies to the prepared baking sheets, spacing them about 1 inch (2.5 cm) apart.

5 Bake the cookies, 1 sheet at a time, until the edges just begin to turn lightly golden, 8–12 minutes. Transfer the baking sheets to wire racks and let the cookies cool on the sheets for 5 minutes, then transfer the cookies to the racks and let cool completely.

 TIP *For coffee-flavored cookies, add 1 teaspoon instant espresso powder to 1 teaspoon hot water, stir to dissolve, and add to the Chocolate Sugar Cookies dough.*

Minty Chocolate Meringues

These pretty cookies use a Swiss meringue, which calls for heating the egg whites and sugar together before beating. It yields a denser, smoother, and more stable meringue than a French meringue, which incorporates the sugar as the whites are beaten. Don't adjust the amount of sugar, as the structure of any meringue depends on the correct ratio of egg whites to sugar.

7 large egg whites

2 cups (1 lb/500 g) sugar

1 teaspoon peppermint extract

5 tablespoons (1 oz/30 g) Dutch-process cocoa powder, sifted

¼ lb (125 g) bittersweet chocolate, finely chopped

¼ lb (125 g) cacao nibs

Makes about 4 dozen cookies

1 Preheat the oven to 350°F (180°C). Line a baking sheet with parchment paper.

2 In a heatproof bowl, whisk together the egg whites and sugar until combined. Set the bowl over (but not touching) barely simmering water in a saucepan and whisk constantly until the sugar is completely dissolved, about 3 minutes. Remove the bowl from the heat and whisk in the peppermint extract.

3 In the bowl of a stand mixer fitted with the whisk attachment, beat the egg white mixture on high speed until stiff, glossy peaks form, about 8 minutes. Stop the mixer and add the cocoa powder, chocolate, and cacao nibs. Gently fold into the meringue until just combined.

4 Drop the meringue by heaping tablespoonfuls onto the prepared baking sheet, spacing the cookies about 1 inch (2.5 cm) apart.

5 Bake until the cookies are dry to the touch and begin to crack, 8–10 minutes. Transfer the baking sheet to a wire rack and let the cookies cool on the sheet for 5 minutes, then transfer the cookies to the rack and let cool completely.

For showstopping Christmas cookies, let the meringues cool completely, then dip in melted chocolate and sprinkle with crushed candy canes. You can also transfer the meringue to a piping bag fitted with a large decorating tip and pipe out intricately shaped cookies.

Gingerbread People

You can add colorful decorations to these classic spice cookies using nonpareils, nonmetallic dragées, small candies, and cylindrical sprinkles. Pipe the icing onto the cookies as directed, then use tweezers to carefully arrange the decorations on the damp icing. A dusting of sanding sugar is also a great choice, as are dried currants and cranberries.

FOR THE COOKIES

5 cups (25 oz/780 g) all-purpose flour, plus more for dusting

1 teaspoon baking soda

½ teaspoon kosher salt

1 tablespoon ground ginger

1 teaspoon ground cinnamon

½ teaspoon ground cloves

1 cup (8 oz/250 g) unsalted butter, at room temperature

½ cup (4 oz/125 g) granulated sugar

½ cup (3½ oz/105 g) firmly packed light brown sugar

1 cup (11 oz/345 g) light molasses

1 large egg

FOR THE ICING

1 cup (4 oz/125 g) confectioners' sugar

2 tablespoons half-and-half

½ teaspoon fresh lemon juice

Makes 2–5 dozen cookies, depending on size

If the icing is too thin, add more confectioners' sugar. If it is too thick, stir in more half-and-half until it reaches the desired consistency.

1 In a large bowl, sift together the flour, baking soda, salt, ginger, cinnamon, and cloves. Set aside.

2 In the bowl of a stand mixer fitted with the paddle attachment, beat together the butter, granulated sugar, and brown sugar on medium speed until light and fluffy, about 3 minutes. Reduce the speed to low and gradually beat in the molasses. Add the egg and beat until combined, about 1 minute. Stop the mixer and scrape down the sides of the bowl. Add the flour mixture and beat on low speed until combined, about 1 minute.

3 Turn the dough out onto a work surface, divide into 4 equal pieces, and shape each into a disk. Wrap separately in plastic wrap and refrigerate for at least 1 hour or up to 2 days. Let the dough soften slightly at room temperature before continuing.

4 Preheat the oven to 400°F (200°C). Line a baking sheet with parchment paper.

5 On a well-floured work surface, roll out 1 dough disk ¼ inch (6 mm) thick. Using gingerbread cookie cutters 3–5 inches (7.5–13 cm) tall, cut out cookies. Transfer the cookies to the prepared baking sheet, spacing them about 1½ inches (4 cm) apart. Repeat with the remaining dough disks. Gather up the scraps of dough, reroll, and cut out more cookies. If the scraps have become sticky, refrigerate for 10 minutes before rerolling. For best results, do not roll the same piece of dough more than twice.

6 Bake until the cookies are lightly browned on the bottom, about 6 minutes. Transfer the baking sheet to a wire rack and let the cookies cool on the sheet for 5 minutes, then transfer the cookies to the rack and let cool completely.

7 Meanwhile, make the icing: In a bowl, whisk together the confectioners' sugar, half-and-half, and lemon juice until completely smooth. Transfer to a piping bag fitted with a fine tip and decorate the cookies as desired.

Almond Cookies

The sliced almonds will color lightly in the oven, intensifying the almond flavor of these simple yet elegant cookies. To add a citrusy note, beat in 2 teaspoons grated orange zest or lemon zest with the almond extract. For a festive touch, dust the cookies with confectioners' sugar.

1⅓ cups (7 oz/220 g)
all-purpose flour

¼ teaspoon baking soda

¼ teaspoon kosher salt

½ cup (4 oz/125 g) unsalted butter,
at room temperature

½ cup (4 oz/125 g) granulated
sugar

1 large egg

1 teaspoon almond extract

½ cup (2 oz/60 g) sliced almonds

Confectioners' sugar, for dusting,
optional

Makes about 2 dozen cookies

1 Preheat the oven to 325°F (165°C). Line a baking sheet with parchment paper.

2 In a bowl, sift together the flour, baking soda, and salt. Set aside.

3 In the bowl of a stand mixer fitted with the paddle attachment, beat together the butter and granulated sugar on medium speed until light and fluffy, about 3 minutes. Reduce the speed to low, add the egg and almond extract, and beat until combined, about 1 minute. Stop the mixer and scrape down the sides of the bowl. Add the flour mixture and beat on low speed until combined, about 1 minute.

4 Shape the dough into 1-inch (2.5-cm) balls and place on the prepared baking sheet, spacing the cookies about 2 inches (5 cm) apart. Using the tines of a fork, gently flatten each ball and press the almonds into the top of the cookies.

5 Bake until the cookies are golden brown on the edges, 12–14 minutes. Transfer the baking sheet to a wire rack and let the cookies cool on the sheet for 3 minutes, then transfer the cookies to the rack and let cool completely. Dust with confectioners' sugar, if using, just before serving.

 Beating the butter for several minutes creates tiny air bubbles, which create structure in the dough and help it rise into a light, fluffy texture.

Spritz Cookies

You will need a cookie press to make these crisp, buttery cookies, a favorite of German bakers at Christmastime. The best presses include a wide selection of plates for creating different shapes, such as a tree, daisy, shell, star, fleur-de-lis, wreath, and snowflake. Choose a press that feels comfortable in your hands.

2 cups (10 oz/315 g)
all-purpose flour

½ teaspoon kosher salt

2 large egg yolks, at room
temperature

2 teaspoons heavy cream

1 teaspoon pure vanilla extract

1 teaspoon almond extract

1 cup (8 oz/250 g) unsalted butter,
at room temperature

⅔ cup (5 oz/155 g) sugar

Makes about 6 dozen cookies

1 Preheat the oven to 375°F (190°C).

2 In a bowl, sift together the flour and salt. In a small bowl, whisk together the egg yolks, cream, and vanilla and almond extracts. Set aside.

3 In the bowl of a stand mixer fitted with the paddle attachment, beat together the butter and sugar on medium speed until light and fluffy, about 3 minutes. Reduce the speed to low, slowly add the egg yolk mixture, and beat until combined, about 1 minute. Stop the mixer and scrape down the sides of the bowl. Add the flour mixture and beat on low speed until combined, about 1 minute.

4 Turn the dough out onto a work surface and knead once or twice to bring it together.

5 Following the manufacturer's instructions, fill the barrel of a cookie press and form cookies onto an ungreased baking sheet, spacing them about 1 inch (2.5 cm) apart. Refrigerate for 10 minutes.

6 Bake until the cookies are light golden brown on the edges, 8–10 minutes. Transfer the cookies to a wire rack and let cool. Repeat with the remaining dough.

 TIP *The key to using a cookie press with ease is the temperature of the dough. If it becomes too warm and soft, refrigerate for 5 minutes before pressing out more cookies. For a festive assortment, add food coloring to the dough or top the cookies with sprinkles after baking.*

Chocolate Sugar Cookies

Here is a delicious sugar cookie for chocolate lovers. You can use either Dutch-process or natural cocoa powder for these cookies. If you prefer a milder chocolate flavor, choose Dutch-process cocoa; for a deeper, more bittersweet flavor, opt for natural cocoa powder. Once the cookies have cooled completely, decorate them with royal icing (page 15), if you like.

2¼ cups (11½ oz/360 g) all-purpose flour, plus more for dusting

⅓ cup (1 oz/30 g) unsweetened cocoa powder or Dutch-process cocoa powder

½ teaspoon baking powder

½ teaspoon baking soda

¼ teaspoon kosher salt

¾ cup (6 oz/185 g) unsalted butter, at room temperature

1 cup (7 oz/220 g) firmly packed light brown sugar

¼ cup (2 oz/60 g) granulated sugar

1 large egg

1 teaspoon pure vanilla extract

Makes about 30 cookies

 To add a simple decorative touch, dip a fork into melted white chocolate and drizzle it over the cooled cookies.

1 In a bowl, sift together the flour, cocoa powder, baking powder, baking soda, and salt. Set aside.

2 In the bowl of a stand mixer fitted with the paddle attachment, beat together the butter, brown sugar, and granulated sugar on medium speed until light and fluffy, about 3 minutes. Reduce the speed to low, add the egg and vanilla, and beat until combined, about 1 minute. Stop the mixer and scrape down the sides of the bowl. Add the flour mixture and beat on low speed until combined, about 1 minute.

3 Turn the dough out onto a work surface and shape into a rough rectangle. Wrap in plastic wrap and refrigerate until firm, at least 1 hour or up to overnight. Before proceeding, let the dough soften slightly at room temperature, about 15 minutes.

4 Preheat the oven to 350°F (180°C). Line a baking sheet with parchment paper.

5 On a lightly floured work surface, using a floured rolling pin, roll out the dough ¼ inch (6 mm) thick. Using cookie cutters, cut out the desired shapes. Transfer the cookies to the prepared baking sheet, spacing them about 1 inch (2.5 cm) apart. Gather up the scraps of dough, reroll, and cut out more cookies.

6 Bake the cookies until they are firm to the touch, 12–15 minutes. Transfer the baking sheet to a wire rack and let the cookies cool on the sheet for 5 minutes, then transfer the cookies to the rack and let cool completely.

Mexican Wedding Cookies

In Mexico, where they are known as polvorones, these melt-in-your-mouth cookies are individually wrapped in tissue paper for serving at weddings and other celebrations. In the United States, similar cookies are called snowballs or Russian tea cakes. To vary the seasoning, replace the cinnamon with ground anise, or omit the spice altogether.

1¾ cups (9 oz/280 g)
all-purpose flour

1 teaspoon ground cinnamon

1 cup (8 oz/250 g) unsalted butter,
at room temperature

1½ cups (6 oz/185 g) confectioners'
sugar

1 teaspoon pure vanilla extract

¼ teaspoon kosher salt

1 cup (5 oz/155 g) coarsely ground
blanched almonds

Makes about 4 dozen cookies

1 Preheat the oven to 350°F (180°C). Line a baking sheet with parchment paper.

2 In a bowl, sift together the flour and cinnamon. Set aside.

3 In the bowl of a stand mixer fitted with the paddle attachment, beat the butter on high speed until fluffy and pale yellow, about 3 minutes. Add ½ cup (2 oz/60 g) of the confectioners' sugar and beat until light and fluffy, about 2 minutes. Reduce the speed to low, add the vanilla and salt, and beat until combined, about 1 minute. Stop the mixer and scrape down the sides of the bowl. Add the flour mixture and beat on low speed until combined, about 1 minute. Stop the mixer and stir in the almonds.

4 Cover the bowl and refrigerate until the dough is chilled but not hard and is no longer sticky to the touch, about 15 minutes.

5 Shape the dough into 1-inch (2.5-cm) balls and place on the prepared baking sheet, spacing the cookies about 1 inch (2.5 cm) apart.

6 Bake until the cookies are just golden on the bottom, 10–12 minutes. Transfer the baking sheet to a wire rack and let the cookies cool on the sheet for 5 minutes.

7 Meanwhile, sift the remaining 1 cup (4 oz/125 g) confectioners' sugar into a shallow bowl. Roll the cookies one at a time in the confectioners' sugar, place on the rack, and let cool completely.

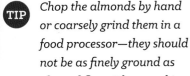

TIP *Chop the almonds by hand or coarsely grind them in a food processor—they should not be as finely ground as almond flour. These cookies are also traditionally made with pecans.*

Honey & Rose Water Mexican Wedding Cookies

This variation of the traditional Mexican wedding cookie omits the cinnamon and replaces it with honey and rose water, giving the cookies a sweet complexity with a light floral note. You can find rose water at well-stocked grocery stores, specialty markets, or online.

1¾ cups (9 oz/280 g)
all-purpose flour

1 cup (8 oz/250 g) unsalted butter,
at room temperature

½ cup (6 oz/185 g) honey

½ teaspoon pure vanilla extract

1 teaspoon rose water

¼ teaspoon kosher salt

1 cup (5 oz/155 g) coarsely ground
blanched almonds

1 cup (4 oz/125 g) confectioners'
sugar

Makes about 4 dozen cookies

1 Preheat the oven to 350°F (180°C). Line a baking sheet with parchment paper.

2 Sift the flour into a bowl. Set aside.

3 In the bowl of a stand mixer fitted with the paddle attachment, beat together the butter and honey on high speed until fluffy and pale yellow, about 3 minutes. Reduce the speed to low, add the vanilla, rose water, and salt, and beat until combined, about 1 minute. Stop the mixer and scrape down the sides of the bowl. Add the flour and beat on low speed until combined, about 1 minute. Stop the mixer and stir in the almonds.

4 Cover the bowl and refrigerate until the dough is chilled but not hard and is no longer sticky to the touch, about 15 minutes.

5 Shape the dough into 1-inch (2.5-cm) balls and place on the prepared baking sheet, spacing the cookies about 1 inch (2.5 cm) apart.

6 Bake until the cookies are just golden on the bottom, 10–12 minutes. Transfer the baking sheet to a wire rack and let the cookies cool on the sheet for 5 minutes.

7 Meanwhile, sift the confectioners' sugar into a shallow bowl. Roll the cookies one at a time in the confectioners' sugar, place on the rack, and let cool completely.

Maple-Pecan Sandies

A relative of shortbread, sand cookies are traditionally laced with pecans, but other nuts—almonds, cashews, macadamias, walnuts—can be substituted. To switch up the flavor and heighten the crunch, stir in about ¾ cup (3 ½ oz/105 g) English toffee bits with the nuts.

2¼ cups (11½ oz/360 g) all-purpose flour

¼ teaspoon kosher salt

2 large egg yolks

3 tablespoons pure maple syrup

½ teaspoon pure vanilla extract

1 cup (8 oz/250 g) unsalted butter, at room temperature

½ cup (4 oz/125 g) granulated sugar

½ cup (3½ oz/105 g) firmly packed light brown sugar

1¼ cups (5 oz/155 g) coarsely chopped pecans

Confectioners' sugar, for dusting

Makes about 3 dozen cookies

1 In a bowl, sift together the flour and salt. In a small bowl, whisk together the egg yolks, maple syrup, and vanilla. Set aside.

2 In the bowl of a stand mixer fitted with the paddle attachment, beat together the butter, granulated sugar, and brown sugar on medium speed until fluffy, about 3 minutes. Reduce the speed to low, slowly add the egg yolk mixture, and beat until combined, about 1 minute. Stop the mixer and scrape down the sides of the bowl. Add the flour mixture and beat on low speed until combined, about 1 minute. Stop the mixer and stir in the pecans.

3 Turn the dough out onto a work surface, divide into 2 equal pieces, and shape each into a log about 6 inches (15 cm) long and 2 inches (5 cm) in diameter. Wrap the pieces separately in plastic wrap and refrigerate for at least 2 hours or up to overnight.

4 Preheat the oven to 325°F (165°C). Line a baking sheet with parchment paper.

5 Cut the logs into ¼-inch (6-mm) slices and transfer to the prepared baking sheet, spacing the cookies about 1½ inches (4 cm) apart.

6 Bake until the cookies are golden brown on the edges and firm to the touch, 15–17 minutes. Transfer the cookies to a wire rack and let cool completely. Dust with confectioners' sugar just before serving.

TIP

For a more intense maple flavor, whisk in 1 teaspoon maple extract with the 3 tablespoons pure maple syrup.

Variation | **Bourbon-Glazed Maple-Pecan Sandies**

Make the dough as directed, whisking 1 tablespoon of bourbon into the egg yolk mixture. Refrigerate and bake as directed. While the cookies are baking, in a saucepan over low heat, whisk together 1 tablespoon bourbon, 3 tablespoons unsalted butter, 6 tablespoons (3¾ oz/115 g) maple syrup, and 2 tablespoons confectioners' sugar. Cook, whisking constantly until the mixture thickens, about 4 minutes. Let the glaze cool slightly, then brush over the top of the warm cookies. Let cool completely, dust with confectioners' sugar, and serve.

Rugelach with Apricot & Pistachio Filling

You can't rush the preparation of these traditional Jewish treats, but you can make them ahead: Freeze the shaped cookies on a baking sheet, transfer to an airtight container, and freeze for up to 1 month. Bake them straight from the freezer, adding a few minutes to the baking time.

FOR THE DOUGH

1 cup (5 oz/155 g) plus
2 tablespoons all-purpose flour,
plus more for dusting

¼ teaspoon kosher salt

½ cup (4 oz/125 g) unsalted butter,
cut into small pieces, at room
temperature

¼ lb (125 g) cream cheese, cut into
small pieces, at room temperature

2 tablespoons granulated sugar

FOR THE FILLING

¾ cup (4½ oz/140 g) dried apricots,
halved

2 tablespoons granulated sugar

¼ teaspoon ground cinnamon

¼ cup (1 oz/30 g) finely chopped
unsalted pistachios, plus more
for sprinkling

1 large egg beaten with 1 teaspoon
water

Turbinado sugar, for sprinkling

Makes 2 dozen cookies

Because this is a sticky dough, you may find it easier to place it between two sheets of waxed paper and then roll it out.

1 To make the dough, in a bowl, sift together the flour and salt. Set aside.

2 In the bowl of a stand mixer fitted with the paddle attachment, beat together the butter and cream cheese on medium speed until smooth and combined, about 3 minutes. Add the granulated sugar and beat until combined, about 2 minutes. Stop the mixer and scrape down the sides of the bowl. Add the flour mixture and beat on low speed until combined, about 1 minute. Turn the dough out onto a floured work surface, divide into 4 equal pieces, and shape each into a disk. Wrap separately in plastic and refrigerate for at least 2 hours or up to 6 hours.

3 Meanwhile, make the filling: In a saucepan over low heat, combine the apricots and ½ cup (125 ml) water. Cover and cook, stirring occasionally, until the fruit absorbs the water, 10–15 minutes. Let cool slightly, then transfer to a food processor and process to a smooth purée. Transfer to a bowl and stir in the granulated sugar, cinnamon, and pistachios. Set aside.

4 Preheat the oven to 350°F (180°C). Line a baking sheet with parchment paper.

5 On a lightly floured work surface, roll out 1 dough disk into a 7-inch (18-cm) circle about ¼ inch (6 mm) thick. Spread ¼ of the filling evenly over the top. Using a large knife, cut the dough into 6 wedges. Starting at the outside edge, gently roll up each wedge toward the point. (If needed, use a thin metal spatula to loosen the wedges from the work surface.) If the dough becomes too soft to roll, refrigerate for about 5 minutes to firm up. Transfer the rolled cookies to the prepared baking sheet, spacing them about 2 inches (5 cm) apart. Repeat with the remaining dough and filling, flouring the work surface as needed. Lightly brush the cookies with the egg mixture, then sprinkle with a pinch each of chopped pistachios and turbinado sugar.

6 Bake until the cookies are golden brown, 18–20 minutes. Transfer the baking sheet to a wire rack and let the cookies cool on the sheet for 5 minutes, then transfer the cookies to the rack and let cool completely.

blackberry-pecan
thumbprints

linzer cookies

peanut butter cookies

perfect chocolate
chip cookies

homemade oreos

seven-layer bars

Index

FAVORITE COOKIES

Conceived and produced by Weldon Owen, Inc.
In collaboration with Williams-Sonoma, Inc.
3250 Van Ness Avenue, San Francisco, CA 94109

Weldon Owen is a division of Bonnier Publishing USA

A WELDON OWEN PRODUCTION

1045 Sansome Street, Suite 100
San Francisco, CA 94111
www.weldonowen.com

Printed and bound in China

First printed in 2016
10 9 8 7 6 5 4 3 2

Library of Congress Cataloging-in-Publication
data is available.

ISBN-13: 978-1-68188-176-8
ISBN-10: 1-68188-176-4

WELDON OWEN, INC.

President & Publisher Roger Shaw
SVP, Sales & Marketing Amy Kaneko
Finance & Operations Director Philip Paulick

Associate Publisher Amy Marr
Project Editor Lesley Bruynesteyn

Creative Director Kelly Booth
Art Director Marisa Kwek
Senior Production Designer Rachel Lopez Metzger

Production Director Chris Hemesath
Associate Production Director Michelle Duggan
Imaging Manager Don Hill

Photographer Annabelle Breakey
Food Stylist Jen Straus
Prop Stylist Glenn Jenkins

ACKNOWLEDGMENTS

Weldon Owen wishes to thank the following people for their generous support
in producing this book: Emily Ayres, Kris Balloun, Debbie Berne,
Gloria Geller, Jackie Hancock, Amy Hatwig, Brad Knilans, Alexis Mersel,
Jonah Podbereski, and Sharon Silva.